Aeroacoustic Testing of Wind Turbine Airfoils

National Renewable Energy Laboratory (NREL)

The BiblioGov Project is an effort to expand awareness of the public documents and records of the U.S. Government via print publications. In broadening the public understanding of government and its work, an enlightened democracy can grow and prosper. Ranging from historic Congressional Bills to the most recent Budget of the United States Government, the BiblioGov Project spans a wealth of government information. These works are now made available through an environmentally friendly, print-on-demand basis, using only what is necessary to meet the required demands of an interested public. We invite you to learn of the records of the U.S. Government, heightening the knowledge and debate that can lead from such publications.

Included are the following Collections:

Budget of The United States Government
Presidential Documents
United States Code
Education Reports from ERIC
GAO Reports
History of Bills
House Rules and Manual
Public and Private Laws

Code of Federal Regulations
Congressional Documents
Economic Indicators
Federal Register
Government Manuals
House Journal
Privacy act Issuances
Statutes at Large

National Renewable Energy Laboratory

A national laboratory of the U.S. Department of Energy
Office of Energy Efficiency & Renewable Energy

Innovation for Our Energy Future

Aeroacoustic Testing of Wind Turbine Airfoils

February 20, 2004 – February 19, 2008

W. Devenport, R.A. Burdisso, H. Camargo,
E. Crede, M. Remillieux, M. Rasnick, and
P. Van Seeters
Virginia Polytechnic Institute and State University
Blacksburg, Virginia

Subcontract Report
NREL/SR-500-43471
May 2010

NREL is operated for DOE by the Alliance for Sustainable Energy, LLC   Contract No. DE-AC36-08-GO28308

Aeroacoustic Testing of Wind Turbine Airfoils

February 20, 2004 – February 19, 2008

W. Devenport, R.A. Burdisso, H. Camargo,
E. Crede, M. Remillieux, M. Rasnick, and
P. Van Seeters
Virginia Polytechnic Institute and State University
Blacksburg, Virginia

NREL Technical Monitor: P. Moriarty
Prepared under Subcontract No. ZAM-4-33226-01

Subcontract Report
NREL/SR-500-43471
May 2010

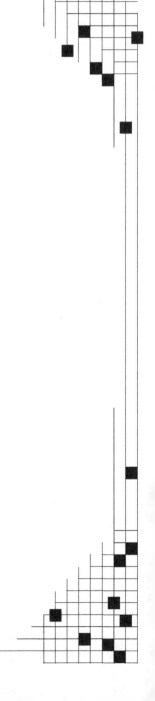

National Renewable Energy Laboratory
1617 Cole Boulevard, Golden, Colorado 80401-3393
303-275-3000 • www.nrel.gov

NREL is a national laboratory of the U.S. Department of Energy
Office of Energy Efficiency and Renewable Energy
Operated by the Alliance for Sustainable Energy, LLC

Contract No. DE-AC36-08-GO28308

Available electronically at http://www.osti.gov/bridge

Available for a processing fee to U.S. Department of Energy
and its contractors, in paper, from:
      U.S. Department of Energy
      Office of Scientific and Technical Information
      P.O. Box 62
      Oak Ridge, TN 37831-0062
      phone: 865.576.8401
      fax: 865.576.5728
      email: mailto:reports@adonis.osti.gov

Available for sale to the public, in paper, from:
      U.S. Department of Commerce
      National Technical Information Service
      5285 Port Royal Road
      Springfield, VA 22161
      phone: 800.553.6847
      fax: 703.605.6900
      email: orders@ntis.fedworld.gov
      online ordering: http://www.ntis.gov/ordering.htm

This publication received minimal editorial review at NREL

 Printed on paper containing at least 50% wastepaper, including 20% postconsumer waste

Foreword

The U.S. Department of Energy (DOE), working through its National Renewable Energy Laboratory (NREL), is engaged in a comprehensive research effort to improve the understanding of wind turbine aeroacoustics. The motivation for this effort is the desire to exploit the large expanse of low wind speed sites that tend to be close to U.S. load centers. Quiet wind turbines are an inducement to widespread deployment, so the goal of NREL's aeroacoustic research is to develop tools that the U.S. wind industry can use in developing and deploying highly efficient, quiet wind turbines at low wind speed sites. NREL's National Wind Technology Center (NWTC) is implementing a multifaceted approach that includes wind tunnel tests, field tests, and theoretical analyses in direct support of low wind speed turbine development by its industry partners. NWTC researchers are working hand in hand with engineers in industry to ensure that research findings are available to support ongoing design decisions.

To that end, wind tunnel aerodynamic tests and aeroacoustic tests have been performed on six airfoils that are candidates for use on small wind turbines. Results are documented in two companion NREL reports.

> Wind Tunnel Aeroacoustic Tests of Six Airfoils for Use on Small Wind Turbines, Stefan Oerlemans, Principal Investigator, the Netherlands National Aerospace Laboratory.

> Wind Tunnel Aerodynamic Tests of Six Airfoils for Use on Small Wind Turbines, Michael Selig, Principal Investigator, University of Illinois at Urbana-Champaign (UIUC).

A similar effort was undertaken for three airfoils that are candidates for use on large wind turbines. Results are reported in the following NREL report and in various conference papers.

> *Aeroacoustic Testing of Wind Turbine Airfoils*, William Devenport and Ricardo Burdisso, Principal Investigators, Virginia Polytechnic Institute and State University.

These reports provide valuable airfoil databases for designers who wish to consider the airfoils tested.[1] Inevitably, however, designers will want to evaluate other airfoils that have not been tested. And not only are wind tunnel tests expensive, it is often difficult to schedule the facilities required within the overall time frame of a project development plan. This dilemma begs the question "Is it really necessary to conduct wind tunnel tests, or can we rely on theoretical predictions?"

Predicting the aeroacoustic emission spectra of a particular airfoil shape is extremely difficult, but predicting the aerodynamic characteristics of a particular airfoil shape is routine practice. Nevertheless, there is always some uncertainty about the accuracy of the predictions in comparison to the results of wind tunnel tests or field performance, and there are questions about the efficacy of two principal airfoil analysis methods: the Eppler and XFOIL codes. To address these

---

[1] The extensive test data discussed in these reports can be provided in electronic format by the NWTC library (303-384-6963).

related issues, at least in part, a theoretical analysis was commissioned of the same airfoils tested in the wind tunnel. The results are documented in the following NREL report.

> *Theoretical Aerodynamic Analyses of Six Airfoils for Use on Small Wind Turbines Using Eppler and XFOIL Codes*, D.M. Somers and M.D. Maughmer, Principal Investigators, Airfoils, Inc.

Possessing both theoretically predicted aerodynamic characteristics and wind tunnel test data for the same six airfoils provides an extraordinary opportunity to compare the performance, measured by energy capture, of wind turbine rotors designed with the different data. This will provide the insight needed to assist designers in deciding whether to pursue wind tunnel tests. Although some differences in the resulting blade planforms (chord and twist distributions) can be expected, a more important question relates to the difference in energy capture and its significance in driving the choices that need to be made during the preliminary design stage. These issues are addressed in a report that compares the differences in Eppler and XFOIL predictions to the UIUC wind tunnel tests and examines the planform and energy capture differences in resulting blade designs.

> *Comparison of Optimized Aerodynamic Performance of Small Wind Turbine Rotors Designed with Theoretically Predicted versus Experimentally Measured Airfoil Characteristics*, Michael Selig, Principal Investigator, University of Illinois at Urbana-Champaign (UIUC).

Another research effort undertaken in support of the U.S. wind turbine industry involves a series of aeroacoustic field tests conducted at the NWTC. Using well documented, consistently applied test procedures, noise spectra were measured for eight small wind turbine configurations. Test results provide valuable information to manufacturers as well as potential users of these turbines. To our knowledge, this is the first comprehensive database of noise data for small wind turbines. The results of this effort are documented in another NREL report.

> *Aeroacoustic Field Tests of Eight Small Wind Turbines,* J. van Dam and A. Huskey, Principal Investigators, NREL's National Wind Technology Center.

Wind tunnel tests, field tests and theoretical analyses provided useful information for development and validation of a semi-empirical noise prediction code developed at NREL. This effort is described in the following reports.

> *Semi-Empirical Aeroacoustic Noise Prediction Code for Wind Turbines,* P. Moriarty and P. Migliore, Principal Investigators, NREL's National Wind Technology Center.

> *Prediction of Turbulent Inflow and Trailing-Edge Noise for Wind Turbines,* P. Moriarty, G. Guidati and P. Migliore, Principal Investigators, NREL subcontracted research.

The codes will be continuously improved, but ultimately could give way to more sophisticated, physics-based computational aeroacoustic codes also being developed by NREL and its subcontractors. For example, researchers at Florida State University (FSU) and the National Aeronautics and Space Administration (NASA) applied modern computational methods to analyze wind turbine blade tip noise. This work was reported in the journal article listed below.

Large-Eddy Simulation of Wing Tip Vortex on Overset Grids, Ali Uzun and Yousuff Hussaini of FSU and Craig Streett of the NASA Langley Research Center, Principal Investigators.

In addition, a comprehensive research effort at the Pennsylvania State University was reported in a series of conference papers and other writings, including:

An Aeroacoustic Analysis of Wind Turbines, Philip Morris, Lyle Long and Ken Brentner, Principal Investigators;

A 3D Parabolic Equation Method for Wind Turbine Noise Propagation in Moving Inhomogeneous Atmosphere, R. Cheng, Philip Morris and Ken Brentner, Principal Investigators;

Rotational Effects on the Aerodynamics and Aeroacoustics of Wind Turbine Airfoils, Steven Miller and Philip Morris, Principal Investigators; and

3-D Time-Accurate Inviscid and Viscous CFD Simulations of Wind Turbine Rotor Flow Fields, Nilay Sezer-Uzol, Ankur Gupta and Lyle Long, Principal Investigators.

Many of the documents described above are published as NREL reports. Some results are presented in various journal articles or conference papers. All of the NREL reports will be available on NREL's Web site at http://www.nrel.gov/publications/. Collectively, these reports represent a significant compendium of information on the aerodynamics and aeroacoustics of contemporary wind turbines.

Clearly, this work represents a significant commitment of DOE resources as well as a significant commitment of personnel over an extended period. We are sure we express the sentiments of all the research participants in saying we sincerely hope the results of these efforts prove beneficial to the wind energy community.

Paul G. Migliore
NREL/NWTC Project Manager, Retired

Patrick Moriarty
NREL/NWTC Project Manager

Acknowledgements

The authors would like to acknowledge the financial support from the National Renewable Energy Laboratory (NREL), in particular Dr. Pat Moriarty and Dr. Paul Migliore, through grant ZAM-4-33226-01. The support of the Office of Naval Research (under grants N00014-05-1-0464 and N00014-04-1-0493) and its technical monitor, Dr. Ronald Joslin also is gratefully acknowledged.

List of Acronyms

CFD	computational fluid dynamics
CMM	coordinate measuring machine
MDF	medium-density fiberboard
NREL	National Renewable Energy Laboratory
SNR	signal-to-noise ratio
SPL	sound pressure level

Table of Contents

List of Figures

List of Tables

1. Introduction

The aeroacoustic noise produced by wind turbines is a significant environmental factor affecting their deployment and operation. Quieter wind turbines can be sited closer to population centers where their power is needed, and can be deployed in greater numbers in such locations. Making such turbines requires not only better physical understanding of the sources and mechanisms of noise production, but also the development of an experimental database of measurements that allows designers to balance aerodynamic and aeroacoustic performance when selecting an airfoil. Additionally, the measurements can be used to improve and validate aeroacoustic prediction methods. One of the principal hurdles in initiating and expanding such a database is the lack of aerodynamic and acoustic data at realistic Reynolds numbers.

The Advanced Turbulent Flow Research Group and the Vibrations and Acoustics Laboratories of Virginia Polytechnic Institute and State University (Virginia Tech) undertook an extensive aerodynamic and acoustic experimental study of three wind turbine airfoils (0.914-m chord) provided by the National Renewable Energy Laboratory (NREL). An NACA 0012 airfoil of the same chord also was tested extensively. The testing took place at the Virginia Tech Stability Wind Tunnel in its newly developed anechoic configuration. The main goal of this research effort was to obtain measurements of the aeroacoustic properties of these airfoils over a range of conditions, providing the foundation of the aeroacoustic database needed by wind-turbine designers. The tests were performed in two tunnel entries, July 2007 and November-December 2007; most of the aerodynamic and acoustic data were collected during the first entry.

For each model, data were collected at various effective angles of attack ranging from zero lift to stall condition (-7° to 14° depending on the airfoil), and various flow speeds ranging from 28 m/s to 66 m/s for nominal chord Reynolds numbers of 1,500,000 to 3,800,000. For certain measurements the model boundary layers were tripped. Researchers conducted aerodynamic flow measurements consisting of static-pressure distributions on the airfoil surfaces, wake-profile measurements downstream of the mid-span of the airfoil, and single hot-wire measurements in the vicinity of the trailing edge. The noise measurements consisted of far-field acoustic data using two 63-microphone phased array systems.

This report is organized into five sections. The facility, aerodynamic and acoustic instrumentation, and the airfoil models are described below in the "Apparatus and Instrumentation" section. The aerodynamic and acoustic results are presented in Section 3 and Section 4, respectively. The last section is a brief summary of the work performed.

2. Apparatus and Instrumentation

This report presents results obtained as the result of two wind tunnel entries conducted during July 2007 and November-December 2007. If changes were made to the apparatus and instrumentation between the entries, then both systems are described. The results associated with each wind tunnel entry are distinguished in the subsequent sections.

2.1. Stability Wind Tunnel
All tests were performed in the Virginia Tech Stability Wind Tunnel. This facility is a continuous, single-return, subsonic wind tunnel with 7.3-m long removable rectangular test

sections of square cross section that is 1.83 m on edge. The general layout is illustrated in Figure 1.

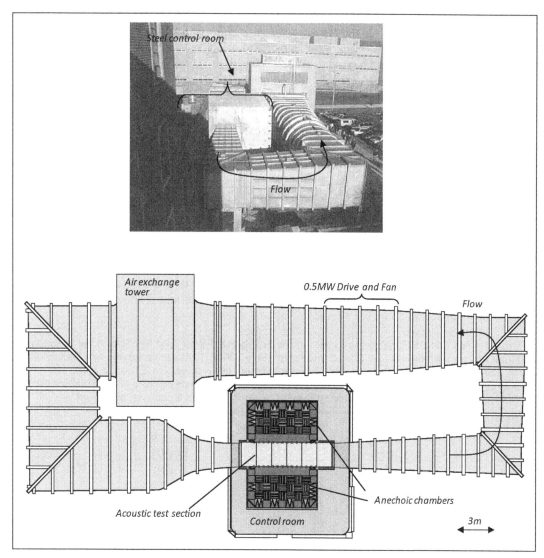

Figure 1. Photograph (a) and plan-view schematic (b) of the Virginia Tech Stability Tunnel in anechoic configuration; photo shows connection to Randolph Hall through metal building at center of picture (a pressure-sealed steel room, containing the test section and operating console)

The tunnel is powered by a 0.45-MW variable-speed DC motor driving a 4.3-m propeller at speeds as great as 600 rpm. This provides a maximum speed in the test section (with no blockage) of about 75 m/s and a Reynolds number per meter up to about 5,000,000. The tunnel forms a closed loop but has an air exchange tower open to the atmosphere to allow for temperature stabilization. The air exchange tower is located downstream of the fan and motor assemblies.

Downstream of the tower, the flow is directed into a 5.5-m × 5.5-m settling chamber containing 7 turbulence-reducing screens each with an open area ratio of 0.6 and separated by 0.15 m. Flow exits this chamber through the 9:1 contraction nozzle, which further reduces turbulence levels and accelerates the flow to test speed. At the downstream end of the test section, flow passes into a 3° diffuser. Sixteen 0.16-m high-vortex generators arranged at intervals of 0.39 m around the floor, walls, and ceiling of the flow path at the entrance to the diffuser serve to mix momentum into the diffuser boundary layer, minimizing the possibility of separation and the consequent instability and inefficiency. The 4 corners in the flow path (2 between the air exchange tower and settling chamber, and 2 between diffuser and fan) are equipped with diagonal arrays of shaped turning vanes. Spacing between the vanes is 0.3 m, except in the corner immediately before the settling chamber where the spacing is 0.076 m.

The test section itself is located in a hermetically sealed steel building (Figure 1). The pressure inside this control room is equalized with the static pressure in the test-section flow, this being below atmospheric by an amount roughly equal to the dynamic pressure. Pressure is equalized through a small aperture in the tunnel sidewall at the upstream entrance to the diffuser.

Flow through the empty test section (measured with a hard-wall test section in place) is both closely uniform and of very low turbulence intensity. Table 1 contains recent (2006) measurements of free-stream turbulence levels as a function of flow speed. Turbulence levels are as low as 0.016% at 12 m/s and increase gradually with flow speed. Choi and Simpson (1987) measured the lateral integral scales of the streamwise velocity in both the horizontal (L_z) and vertical (L_y) directions. They found $L_z = 56$ mm for 15 m/s and 28 mm for 37.5 m/s, and $L_y = 122$ mm for 15 m/s and 25 mm for 37.5 m/s.

Table 1. Free-Stream Turbulence Levels in the Empty Hard-Wall Test Section of the Stability Tunnel as a Function of Flow Speed (measured May 2006); Turbulence Levels Are Based on Spectral Integrations that Exclude Electrical Noise at Frequencies Exceeding 100 Hz; Low Frequency Cut-Off is Selected to Remove Obvious Flow Unsteadiness (When the Spectrum Inflects), and High-Frequency Cut-Off is Chosen at the Spectrum Minimum

Freestream Velocity V [m/s]	RMS Streamwise Fluctuations u'/V	Frequency Range fR [Hz]
12	0.016%	7–250
21	0.021%	24–725
30	0.024%	33–2,186
48	0.029%	40–3,641
57	0.031%	75–5,112

2.2. Anechoic System
2.2.1. Physical Layout
The Stability Wind Tunnel is unique in that it has an anechoic system that can be installed and removed as needed. The anechoic system permits acoustic as well as aerodynamic flow measurements and was used for all tests reported here. The anechoic system consists of an acoustic test section flanked by 2 anechoic chambers (Figure 1, Figure 2, Figure 3).

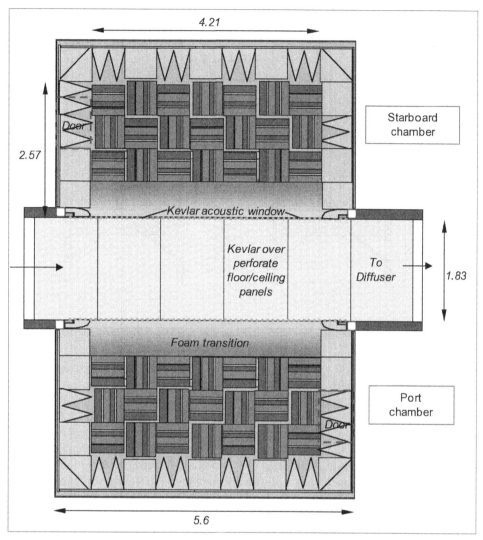

Figure 2. Plan view cross-section of the anechoic system as installed, showing the test section flanked by the two anechoic chambers (dimensions in meters); areas of the test-section sidewalls that are acoustically treated are shown in blue

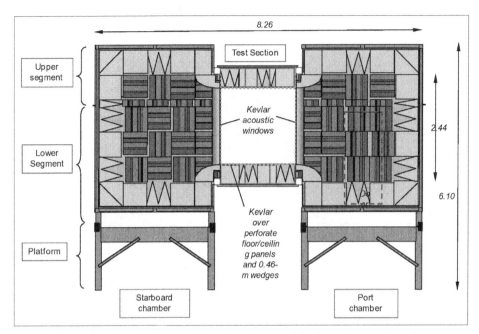

Figure 3. Cross section of the anechoic chambers and test section looking downstream (dimensions in meters)

The acoustic test section is shown in Figure 2 to Figure 7. The test section consists of acoustically treated upper and lower walls that run the full 7.3-m length of the test section and partial sidewalls (also treated) at the test-section entrance and exit. Large rectangular openings in the sidewalls which extend 4.2 m in the streamwise direction and cover the full 1.83-m height of the test section serve as acoustic windows (Figure 4). Sound generated in the test flow exits the test section through these into the anechoic chambers to either side. Large tensioned panels of Kevlar cloth cover these openings, permitting the sound to pass and containing the bulk of the flow. The test-section arrangement thus acoustically simulates a half-open jet. The Kevlar windows eliminate the need for a jet catcher and, by containing the flow, substantially reduce the lift interference when airfoil models are placed into the test flow. This arrangement is unique to the Virginia Tech Stability Wind Tunnel and, like the anechoic system itself, is a relatively recent innovation.

Figure 4. Exterior view of the anechoic test section with the acoustic windows and the port side anechoic chamber removed; starboard-side anechoic chamber visible in the background

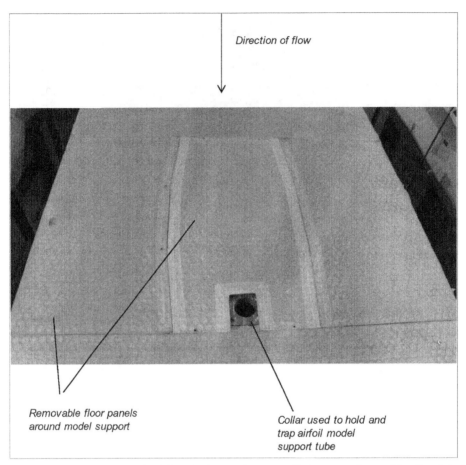

Direction of flow

Removable floor panels around model support

Collar used to hold and trap airfoil model support tube

Figure 5. View of the lower wall of the wind tunnel test section, as configured for the July 2007 entry, showing the collar used to hold one end of the airfoil support tube (note that the Kevlar acoustic windows that form the sidewalls of this part of the test section have been removed)

The upper wall of the test section is formed from a series of perforated steel-sheet panels bonded to a layer of Kevlar cloth, forming a smooth, quiet, but acoustically transparent flow surface. The volume behind this flow surface is filled with 0.457-m–high foam wedges that eliminate any acoustic reflections at frequencies greater than 190 Hz. For the two wind-tunnel entries reported here, the construction of the lower wall of the test section was the same as the upper wall with one exception. For the November-December entry, a 1.83-m × 0.84-m section of the acoustically treated lower wall immediately around the model mount was replaced by medium-density fiberboard (MDF) panels (Figure 7, Figure 8). The MDF panels can be removed and replaced, this provides access through which models can be installed more easily. The partial sidewalls (Figure 2) include 150-mm deep acoustic absorbers filled with a combination of melamine foam and fiberglass insulation and covered with a tensioned Kevlar flow surface.

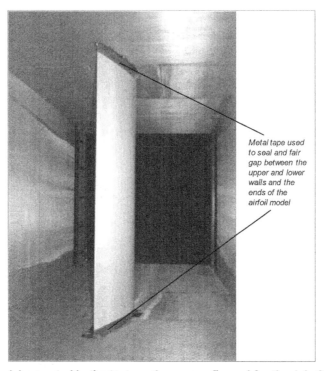

Metal tape used to seal and fair gap between the upper and lower walls and the ends of the airfoil model

Figure 6. Airfoil model mounted in the test section as configured for the July 2007 entry, as seen from downstream; identical support and panel arrangements are used on the lower and upper walls

Figure 7. Airfoil model mounted in the test section as configured for the November-December 2007 entry, as seen from downstream (note the end plates on airfoil model and the partially installed trailing-edge hot-wire traverse)

The upper and lower walls contain hardware for the (vertical) mounting of two-dimensional airfoil models. For the July 2007 entry, simple split-aluminum collars located just below the test section floor and just above its ceiling were used to hold—and trap at a given angle—an 88.9-mm diameter airfoil-model support tube (*see* Figure 5, Figure 6). The collars were mounted using steel beams embedded in the upper and lower walls to the test section structure. The same collar assembly was used at the upper wall of the test section for the November-December entry. At the lower wall, however, a more-sophisticated bearing system was employed (Figure 9). The bearing system was designed to fit the same 88.9-mm tube, but allowed for the more rapid installation and removal of models and easier rotation to angle of attack.

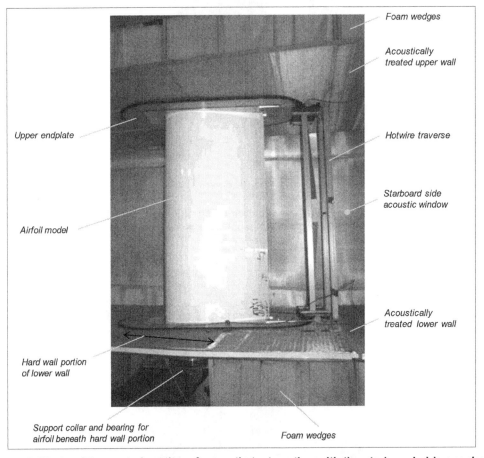

Figure 8. Photo of the central portion of acoustic test section with the starboard-side anechoic chamber and Kevlar acoustic window removed (the port-side acoustic window); an airfoil model installed with end plates and the trailing-edge hot-wire traverse are visible

Both mounting systems place the axis of the mounting tube midway between the acoustic windows (i.e., test-section sidewalls) and 3.56 m from the upstream end of the test section. To date, all airfoil models tested in the anechoic test section have been built to completely span the vertical height of the test section with a tube of this size protruding from both spanwise ends.

The axis of the tube—and thus the axis of rotation—of the model is located one quarter of the distance from the leading to trailing edge.

Hard wall portion of lower test section wall

Support collar for airfoil model

Bearing used to control rotation to angle of attack

Airfoil pressure tubing

Figure 9. Photo matching Figure 5, but taken from beneath the test section showing the collar and bearing arrangement that form the airfoil-mount bearing arrangement

Plain-weave Kevlar 120 cloth (7.9 grams/m^2) is used to form the acoustic windows. This use of the material was pioneered by Jaeger et al. (2000). They investigated different means of shielding a phased-array microphone system embedded in the wall of a test section. They found that, up to at least 25 kHz, this cloth transmits sound with very little attenuation. The Stability Tunnel is the first anechoic wind tunnel to employ this technology on a facility scale. The Kevlar cloth forming the acoustic windows is stretched on a 5.37-m × 2.51-m tensioning frame to a tension of the order of 0.5 tonnes per linear meter. The Kevlar windows are sewn from 3 lengths of Kevlar cloth. When mounted, the two 40-mm-wide seams run streamwise along the test section 0.19 m to 0.28 m below the upper wall and a similar distance above the lower wall.

Two anechoic chambers are positioned on either side of the test section (Figure 2, Figure 3, Figure 4). Each chamber extends 5.6 m in the streamwise direction. The internal width of each chamber is 2.6 m (out from the test section acoustic window), and the internal length is 4.2 m in the streamwise direction. The chamber walls are constructed from medium density fiberboard (MDF) supported by a network of external steel beams, and are lined internally with 0.610-m-high acoustic foam wedges that eliminate acoustic reflections at frequencies greater than 140 Hz. Quarter-elliptical foam sections surround the acoustic windows so as to form a smooth transition between the lower and upper walls of the test section on the inside of the windows, and the acoustically treated walls of the anechoic chambers on the outside of the acoustic windows. The chamber sections are designed to seal to the sides of the test section and minimize (if not eliminate) any net flow through either acoustic window.

2.2.2. Calibration Information

The anechoic system was constructed and installed in the Stability Wind Tunnel in 2006. Work on the system, the acoustic treatment of the rest of the tunnel circuit, and the calibration of the facility is ongoing. Details of the calibration are given in Crede (2008), Staubs (2008), Remillieux, Camargo, Burdisso (2007), and Remillieux et al. (2008), and are summarized here. Figure 10 shows empty test-section background sound pressure levels (SPL) in the starboard-side anechoic chamber as a function of flow speed. Noise levels in the port-side chamber are nearly identical. These measurements were made 1.9 m from the center of the starboard-side acoustic window using a single 12.7-mm diameter B&K microphone. Note that at the slowest speed (11.2 m/s) the tunnel is quiet enough that the spectrum is dominated by the electrical noise of the microphone system and thus, in this specific case, the overall shape of this spectrum should not be taken as an indicator of actual acoustic levels. Background noise levels that are less than 200 Hz mostly are associated with fan tones. Background noise levels greater than 200 Hz primarily are broadband and believed to be due to a combination of noise sources including the fan, turning vanes, and scrubbing noise from flow surfaces in and around the test section.

11

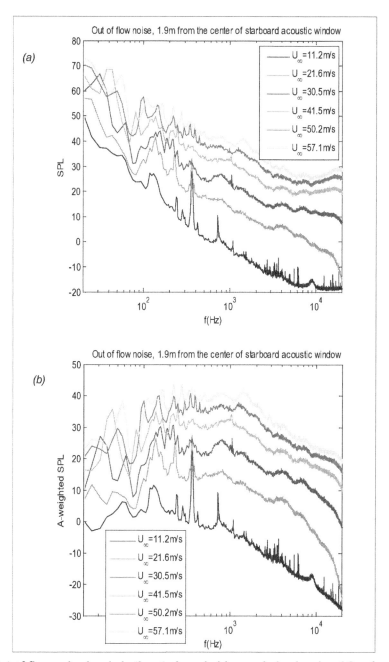

Figure 10. Out-of-flow noise levels in the starboard-side anechoic chamber 1.9 m from the center of the acoustic window (2.7 m from the test-section center) as a function of flow speed in the empty test section (a) 1-Hz bandwidth SPL, and (b) 1-Hz bandwidth A-weighted SPL

In an effort to accurately determine the absolute noise levels of the model tested, an initial procedure for amplitude calibration of the microphone phased array was developed for this new facility. In addition to determining the array sensitivity, corrections were made to account for the noise-attenuation effects of the Kevlar and the shear layer by Remillieux et al. (2007). The correction factors to account for the loss through the shear layer and the Kevlar window must be added to the array output. That is:

$$SPL_{True} \text{ (dB)} = SPL_{Measured} + \Delta_K + \Delta_F.$$

Where the actual level at the array position is SPL_{True} (dB), the array output is $SPL_{Measured}$ and Δ_K and Δ_F denote the corrections for the losses through the Kevlar window and the flow effects, respectively.

Figure 11(a) and (b) shows the corrections Δ_K and Δ_F as a function of frequency in one-third octave bands. In these figures, a positive value of the curve indicates a loss (in decibels). Due to the small noise source used in this calibration, results that are less than 2,500 Hz are not very reliable. In Figure 11(a), the losses through the Kevlar window should converge to zero at low frequencies, and thus the results were curve fitted (dashed line). Figure 11(b) depicts the losses due to the boundary layer at Mach 0.12 (solid curve), Mach 0.15 (dashed curve), and Mach 0.17 (smaller-dashed curve) as a function of frequency. The results indicate a weak dependence of the losses with frequency while increasing with flow speed.

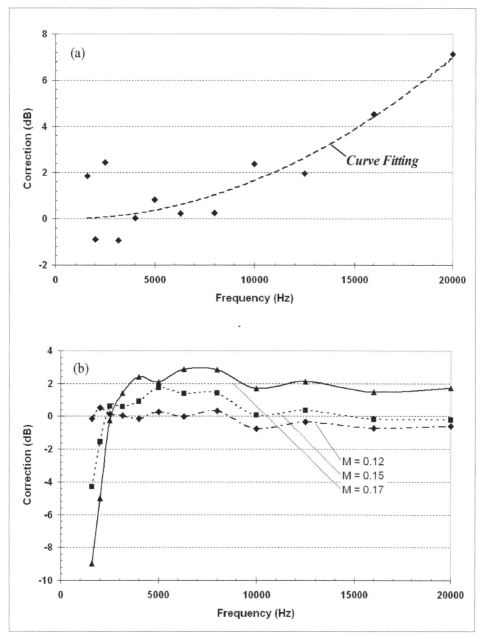

Figure 11. Attenuation of sound passing through the (a) acoustic Kevlar windows and (b) boundary layer as a function of frequency in one-third octave bands

Figure 12 shows sample mean pressure measurements made on a 0.91-m chord NACA 0012 airfoil positioned in the test-section center at an angle of attack of 10.3°. The pressure distribution closely matches panel-method predictions for an angle of attack of 8.1°, suggesting an interference correction of -22%. A consistent correction is seen at other flow speeds, angles of attack, and with other airfoils of the same chord length.

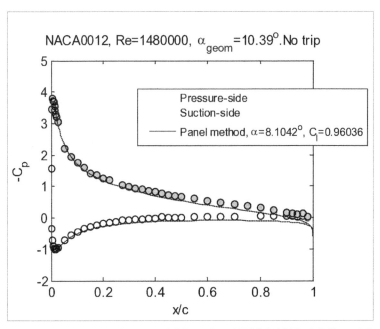

Figure 12. Mean pressure distribution on a 0.91-m chord NACA 0012 airfoil model positioned at the same location as the airfoils in the current test and at a geometric angle of attack of 10.4°

Consistent with this, a detailed comparison of the measured and predicted pressure distributions along with panel-method simulations shows no sign of any camber correction, implying that the effects of the Kevlar windows on the airfoil flow are confined to the aerodynamic far field. The interference correction is a result of the slight residual flow through the Kevlar windows and the windows' deflection under the pressure load imposed by flow field around the airfoil. Direct measurements show the windows' deflection increasing with flow speed and airfoil angle of attack. When the NACA 0012 airfoil is at this angle of attack and with a flow speed of 28 m/s, the maximum deflection is close to 40 mm. Pressure-difference measurements suggest a maximum flow velocity through the Kevlar windows of between 5% and 10% of the free-stream velocity when under this condition. Boundary-layer measurements on the test-section walls show a boundary-layer thickness of about 100 mm at the downstream end of the windows with no model present, and a thickness of about 135 mm for the NACA 0012 model at 0° angle of attack. As with all closed-section tunnels, the blockage associated with a model, the viscous wake it sheds, and any viscous flows it produces at the walls of the test section, result in some acceleration of free-stream flow between the test-section entrance and exit. When the NACA 0012 model is at 8° effective angle of attack, this acceleration increases the free-stream velocity by about 3.5% from the entrance to the exit of the test section.

2.3. Airfoil Models
Aerodynamic and acoustic measurements were performed on 4 airfoil models with NACA 0012, Risø B1-18, DU96, and S831 (developed by NREL) sections. Section shapes, except for the proprietary B1-18 airfoil, are shown in Figure 13, which also includes a comparison of airfoil thicknesses and leading-edge radii. Note that, with the exception of the NACA 0012, all the

airfoils are 18% thick. Leading-edge radii vary by a factor of 5, however, from the very sharp leading edge of the S831 (0.42% chord radius) to the rounded B1-18 (2.19% chord radius).

The models, constructed by Novakinetics LLC, were designed to span the complete vertical height of the test section. These models have a 1.8-m span and 914-mm chord, and are built around 88.9-mm diameter steel tube that forms a spar centered on the quarter-chord location. The models have fiberglass composite skin and a fill of fiberboard and polyurethane foam. The steel tube projects 166 mm past the ends of each airfoil and was used for mounting. Novakinetics proof tested the NACA 0012 model to a load of 27 kN evenly distributed across the span—this being much greater than the maximum expected aerodynamic load. Deflection at this load at center span was approximately 5 mm.

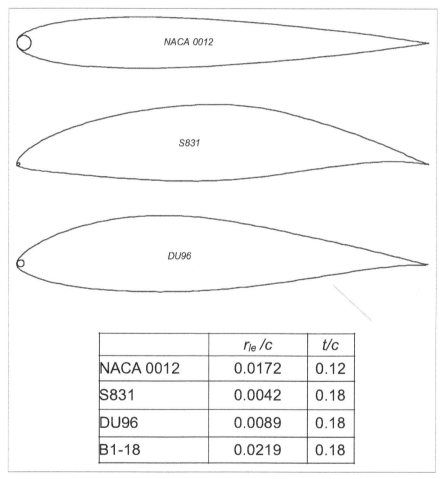

	r_{le}/c	t/c
NACA 0012	0.0172	0.12
S831	0.0042	0.18
DU96	0.0089	0.18
B1-18	0.0219	0.18

Figure 13. Comparison of airfoil section shapes (to scale), circles at the leading edges show leading-edge radius; table compares leading-edge radius and thickness to chord ratios

Models were instrumented with approximately 80 pressure taps having 0.5-mm internal diameter located near the mid-span. The nominal chordwise locations of the pressure taps were the same on all the airfoils and on both sides of each airfoil (listed in Table 2). The taps appeared free from burrs and other defects. The taps were connected internally to 1.6-mm Tygon tubing that exited the model through the center of the steel tube. To provide access to the interior of the model in the area of the pressure taps, a hatch was provided on one side of the model and fixed in place by countersinking a series of flathead bolts into the airfoil surface. Both bolt heads and the slight step at the edge of hatch were covered with 0.05-mm Scotch tape during testing.

Table 2. Nominal Chordwise Locations (x/c) of Pressure Taps on Both Sides of the Airfoil Models

0.00E+00	7.50E-02	3.50E-01	7.50E-01
2.50E-03	1.00E-01	3.75E-01	8.00E-01
5.00E-03	1.25E-01	4.00E-01	8.50E-01
7.50E-03	1.50E-01	4.25E-01	9.00E-01
1.00E-02	1.75E-01	4.50E-01	9.20E-01
1.25E-02	2.00E-01	4.75E-01	9.40E-01
1.50E-02	2.25E-01	5.00E-01	9.60E-01
1.75E-02	2.50E-01	5.50E-01	9.80E-01
2.00E-02	2.75E-01	6.00E-01	
2.50E-02	3.00E-01	6.50E-01	
5.00E-02	3.25E-01	7.00E-01	

A coordinate measuring machine (CMM), manufactured by FARO (Fusion model) was used to compare the machined profile shapes provided by Novakinetics to the model airfoils. Measurements were made at 4 locations across the span (¼ span, midspan, ¾ span, and at the pressure taps access hatch). Measurements showed maximum deviations of 5 mm (0.6% chord) from the design profiles. Pressure tap locations were also measured. A standard linear vortex panel method, similar to that described by Kuethe and Chow (1986), was used to investigate the influence of these geometry variations on the pressure distributions. The panel method results, as well as all the CMM measurements are reported in Appendix A.

During testing the airfoil models were mounted vertically in the test section (as shown in Figure 6 and Figure 7), with the leading edge 3.33 m downstream of the test section entrance and perpendicular to the oncoming flow. For the July 2007 wind tunnel entry (Figure 6), the gaps between the ends of the model and the upper and lower test-section walls were covered and faired using aluminum foil tape. Support for the tape over the larger gap at the upper wall was provided by acoustic foam pieces—cut to the airfoil profile—that were placed into the gap before tape was applied. For the November-December tunnel entry tape was not used, and instead end plates were attached to both ends of the model (Figure 7). These plates were 1.68-m long in the chordwise direction, 0.66-m wide, and had semicircular ends of radius 0.33 m. The plates were attached to the ends of the model and rotated with it to the angle of attack. At the edges of the endplates, the roughly 20-mm step to the surrounding wind tunnel wall was faired using closed-cell foam strips with a quarter-circle cross section mounted around the periphery of the end plates. The end plates reduced noise and improved the aerodynamics of the flow generated at the junctions between the airfoil models and upper and lower walls.

The zero geometric angle of attack of the models was determined using the measured pressure distribution, and is discussed below. For the July 2007 entry, angles relative to zero were

17

determined by measuring the location of the trailing edge on the lower wall of the test section. For the November-December entry, relative angles were set by using a lever arm and scale arrangement attached to the bearing below the test section. The accuracy of changes in angle of attack was estimated to be ±0.3° in both cases.

For certain measurements, the model boundary layers were tripped to ensure a stable and spanwise uniform transition location and a fully turbulent boundary layer at the trailing edge. Two different types of trip were used. The first, fabricated from serrated trip tape (Glasfaser-Flugzeug-Service GmbH 3D Turbulator Tape), was applied along the entire span with its leading edge at the 5% chord location on the airfoil suction side, and at the 10% chord location on the pressure side. The tape has a thickness of 0.5 mm and is 12 mm in overall width. The leading and trailing edges were cut to form aligned serrated edges with a 6-mm distance between points. The second consisted of a random distribution of Number 60 silicon carbide grit particles, applied in a 100-mm-wide spanwise band centered on the leading edge. The grit size and pattern were designed to simulate a soiling of the airfoil leading edge caused by insects. The trip was fabricated on 100-mm-wide 0.1-mm-thick double-sided tape. Grit was applied to one side of the tape using a template manufactured by NREL so as to provide a repeatable panel, the other side of the tape then was smoothly applied to the model. Figure 14 shows this "soiled" trip applied to the leading edge of one of the airfoil models. The density of grit locations is about 5 per square centimeter near the leading edge, and 1.5 per square centimeter near the edge of the trip. Note that, when applied, the soiled trip covered only the middle half-span of the airfoil models.

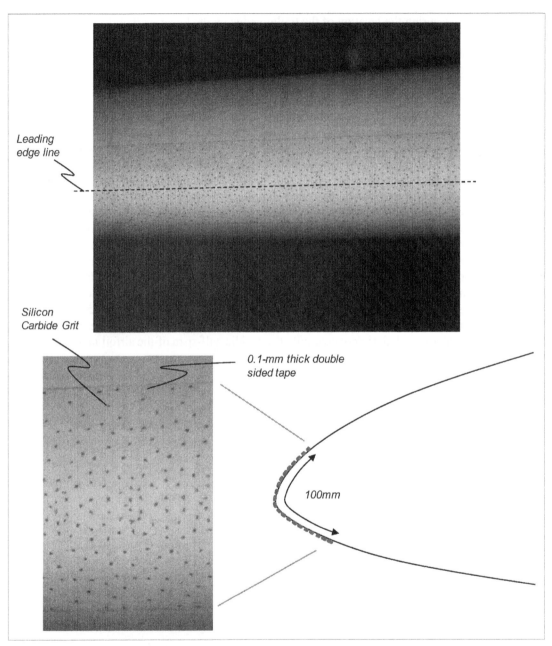

Leading edge line

Silicon Carbide Grit

0.1-mm thick double sided tape

100mm

Figure 14. "Soiled" trip applied to the leading edge of the DU96 airfoil; top shows wide-angle view of leading edge looking downstream, bottom shows detail of the leading edge with a schematic cross section showing the region of application

2.4. Aerodynamic Instrumentation
2.4.1. Reference Conditions

During all measurements, various tunnel flow conditions were monitored. Flow speed was monitored using an 8-mm diameter reference Pitot static probe located near the exit of the

19

contraction. The probe was positioned 0.035 m upstream of the test-section entrance, 1.22 m from the floor, and 0.23 m from the port-side wall. The free-stream dynamic pressure was sensed using a Setra Model 239 pressure transducer. Temperature in the test section was monitored using an Omega Thermistor type 44004 (accuracy $\pm0.2°C$) and the ambient absolute pressure was determined using a Validyne DB-99 Digital Barometer (resolution 0.01" Hg).

2.4.2. Airfoil Pressure Distributions

A series of Setra model 239 pressure transducers (with ranges of ±7.5" H_2O, ±15" H_2O, and ±2.5 psi) were used to measure static pressures on the airfoil surfaces. These transducers were zeroed and calibrated against each other to minimize errors associated with difference in offset and sensitivity. Pressures from the taps on the airfoil model surfaces were directed through a Scanivalve system for measurement. The pressure from each tap—converted to voltage by the transducer—was measured simultaneously with the reference dynamic pressure, using a 16-bit Agilent E1432 Digitizer. After switching the Scanivalve and allowing the pressure to settle for 0.5 seconds, 5 records of 1,024 samples were measured at a sampling rate of 3,200 Hz, over a total sampling time of 3 seconds, to determine the mean pressure.

2.4.3. Airfoil Wake Measurements

The two-axis wind tunnel traverse shown in Figure 15 was used to position wake probes in the test section. To determine airfoil drag, wake profiles were measured downstream of the mid-span of the airfoil models at $X/c = 3.74$. The traverse was mounted inside the test section and produced an overall solid blockage of about 10%. Probes were mounted well upstream of the traverse to avoid the region of flow acceleration associated with the blockage. Wake profiles were measured using a rake of 5 Dwyer model 160 Pitot–static probes. These 3.18-mm diameter probes—which normally include a 90° bend—were specially made in the straight configuration shown in Figure 16. The 5 probes were held at 25.4-mm intervals across the flow using the bracket shown in Figure 17. The bracket, in turn, was held using a 32-mm diameter sting attached to the traverse gear. Total distance from the upstream end of the traverse to the tips of the probes was close to 1.4 m, the probe tips being approximately 340 mm upstream of the bracket. To prevent relative movement of the probe tips a thin spacer (made of aluminum tape) was used to tie the probes together between 100 mm and 150 mm from the probe tips.

Ten Omega Model PX277-30D5V pressure transducers set to a range of ±7.5 in of water were used to sense the pressures from the 5 probes relative to the wind tunnel free-stream static pressure. Voltage outputs from the 10 transducers along with that from the wind tunnel reference transducer were recorded using the 16-bit Agilent E1432 Digitizer (described above). A single Agilent VEE program was used to control the data acquisition, the traverse position, and the data processing and saving. The 5 stagnation and 5 static-pressure coefficients sensed by the probe rake were calculated by averaging 30,000 samples of the pressure transducer outputs recorded at a rate of 3,200 Hz. To set the transducer offsets, profile measurements were made with no flow before each rake occurred. For the July 2007 entry, measurements were made with the probe rake oriented in the spanwise direction so as to simultaneously measure 5 profiles at slightly different spanwise stations. During the November-December entry, measurements were made with the probe rake oriented perpendicular to the span so that the 5 probes simultaneously recorded pressures from 5 different positions across the same wake profile, minimizing the number of profile points needed.

Figure 15. Photograph of the traverse gear mounted in the anechoic test section (looking upstream)

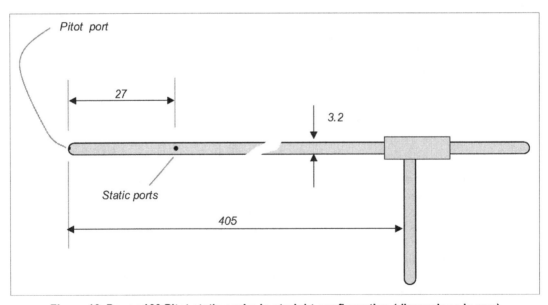

Figure 16. Dwyer 160 Pitot static probe in straight configuration (dimensions in mm)

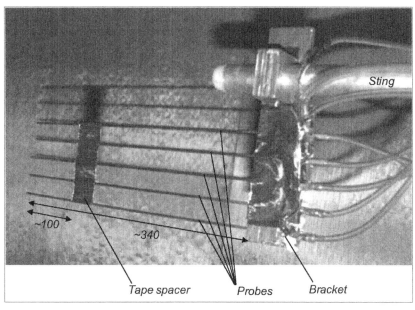

Figure 17. Pitot static-probe rake detail (dimensions in mm)

2.4.4. Hot-Wire Anemometry

Hot-wire profiles were measured in the vicinity of the trailing edge of the B1-18, DU96, and S831 airfoils using single hot-wire probes. These measurements all were made as part of the November-December 2007 entry. The probes were positioned using the specially built traverse shown in Figure 18.

The traverse was powered by 2 synchronized stepper-motor driven linear stages mounted to the airfoil endplates downstream of the trailing edge. Probes were held using a 12.7-mm thick strut mounted across the airfoil span some 330 mm downstream of its trailing edge. The strut connected the 2 stages and traversed with them. A single angle bracket rigidly held the 4.6-mm diameter hot-wire probe stem positioning the hot-wire at mid-span immediately downstream of the trailing edge. Additional diagonal beams (also 12.7-mm thick) attached to the strut above and below the probe (*see* Figure 18) and connected to the stages added rigidity to the probe support to minimize vibration. A further non-traversing 25.4-mm-thick strut with rounded leading and trailing edges was attached 180 mm downstream of the probe support, fixing the distance between the stages. The entire assembly rotated to angle of attack with the airfoil and endplates. One shortcoming of this traverse arrangement was that the traverse structure experiences an unsteady loading when the airfoil wake impinges on one or both of the spanwise struts. This loading could lead to probe vibration. Although this vibration could not be observed directly (probes were monitored using a video camera located on the test-section wall), there is some evidence in spectral measurements made at certain conditions. This evidence is discussed below, along with the presentation of results.

A straight-type single hot-wire probe, either an Auspex AHWU-100 or a TSI type 1210-T1.5, was used for all measurements. Probes were balanced and operated using a Dantec 90C10 Streamline Bridge System and used to obtain mean velocity, turbulence quantities, and spectra.

The Agilent E1432 16-bit digitizer was used for data acquisition. Hot-wire calibration, traversing, and the data acquisition all were controlled using Agilent VEE programs written at Virginia Tech. Flow temperature was monitored continuously during hot-wire measurements, and corrections were made using the method developed by Bearman (1971).

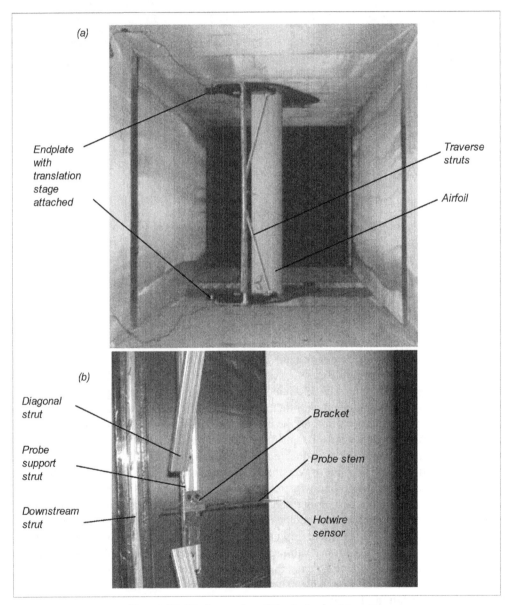

Figure 18. Photographs of the hot-wire traverse

Hot-wire measurements were used to reveal the flow and turbulence structure in the trailing-edge boundary layer relative to the local-edge velocity (defined as 98% of the free-stream velocity), rather than in absolute terms. For this reason hot-wire probes could be calibrated by positioning them in the potential flow region outside the airfoil boundary layer (saving much test time). In this case, the hot-wire was calibrated by determining its output voltage as a function of the tunnel free-stream speed, and fitting this to King's law of convective heat transfer with an exponent of 0.45. King's Law assumes that the correlation between the convective heat loss of a hot-wire and the flow velocity are related:

$$E^2 = A + Bu^n$$

where E is the sensor voltage, u the velocity, n the exponent, and A, B are constants.

Although the flow speed at the calibration points was not equal to the tunnel free stream, speeds were expected to be closely proportional. In effect, this means that subsequent hot-wire velocity and turbulence measurements (after dividing by the tunnel free-stream velocity) were obtained normalized on the velocity at the calibration point U_{cal}. Except for conditions where no boundary-layer edge could be observed (such as stall), data subsequently were renormalized on the observed edge velocity U_e.

Each boundary-layer hot-wire profile consisted of measurements at some 40 points, typically covering about 60 mm in the direction normal to the trailing edge. At most points, mean velocity and turbulence intensity were obtained by averaging approximately 20 records each of 1,024 points measured at a rate of 3,200 Hz. At every fifth point, 50 records of 1,024 points were recorded at a rate of 51,200 Hz, so that low-uncertainty velocity spectra also could be calculated.

2.5. Acoustic Instrumentation

Acoustic data were collected using 2 microphone phased arrays (shown in Figure 19). The equal-aperture spiral was used in the July tunnel entry and the star array in the November-December tunnel entry. Both arrays have 63 microphones arranged in 7 arms with 9 microphones per arm. The inside and outside diameters are 0.25 m and 1.5 m for the star array and the equal-aperture spiral has diameters of 0.1 m and 1.47 m, respectively. The array patterns are shown in Figure 20. The array center bodies have a laser pointer that projects a laser dot along a line perpendicular to the array plane passing through the array origin. This laser pointer is used for alignment purposes. Both arrays have the same type of microphones and signal conditioning. The microphones are Panasonic WM-60AY Electret and have a flat frequency response in the 200 Hz to 18,000 Hz range. The microphone signal rolls off steeply at 18 kHz. The microphone signal conditioning has a high-pass filter with a corner frequency of approximately 200 Hz. A key difference between these arrays is in the microphone structural mounting. In the equal-aperture spiral array the microphones are mounted on a very stiff honeycomb plate, and the star array uses carbon-composite tubes. The acoustically reflective surface of the equal-aperture spiral array results in a doubling of the microphone signals. To compare the results between the arrays, the output levels of the equal-aperture array must be reduced by 6 dB.

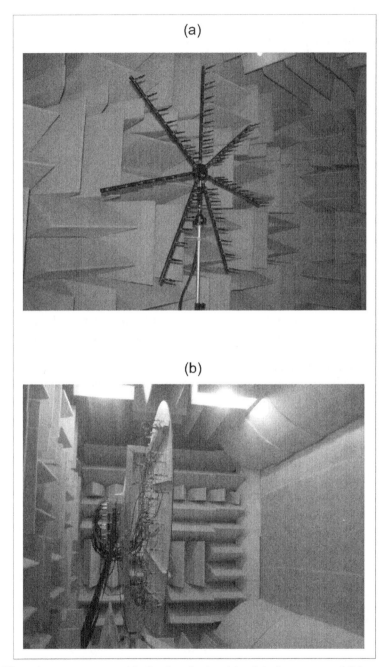

(a)

(b)

Figure 19. Microphone arrays used in the two test entries (a) star array and (b) equal-aperture spiral array

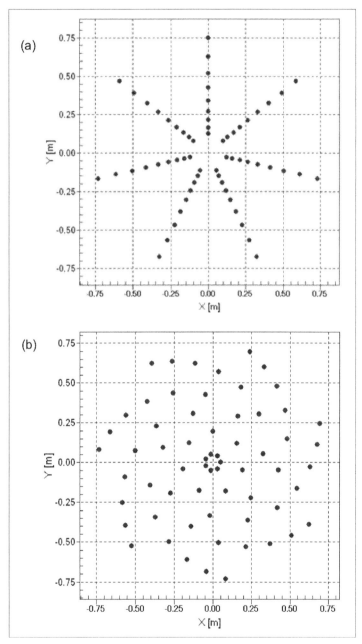

Figure 20. Microphone phased-array patterns

The resolution and signal-to-noise ratio (SNR) of the arrays were determined by computing the point-spread function for all the one-twelfth octave bands in the 500 Hz to 5,000 Hz frequency range. The resolution and SNR as a function of the frequency for a plane 3 m from the array are shown for each array in Figure 21. The plots show differences between the arrays. The resolution for the equal-aperture spiral array is slightly better than for the star array. The SNR data shows that the equal-aperture array is better at frequencies below 2,000 Hz and the star array is better above this frequency.

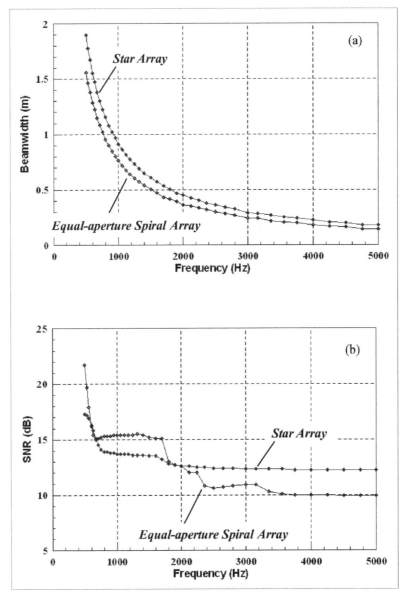

Figure 21. Array (a) resolution or beamwidth and (b) signal-to-noise ratio in one-twelfth octave bands for the 500 Hz to 5,000 Hz frequency range at a distance of 3.0 m; flow in the tunnel section is not accounted for in these results

For illustrative purposes, the array point-spread function for the star array at a distance of 3.0 m from the arrays is plotted in Figure 22 for 4 one-twelfth octave bands in the frequency range of interest. For comparison, the size of the models (1-m chord) is shown in Figure 22(a), where it is clear that the spot size at the 542.4-Hz band is larger than for the airfoil chord. Thus, the noise sources in the acoustic maps below this band would appear larger than the size of the airfoil. This would make the identification of the noise source location very difficult. Additionally, the computation of the trailing-edge noise spectrum by integration over the trailing-edge region would be inaccurate.

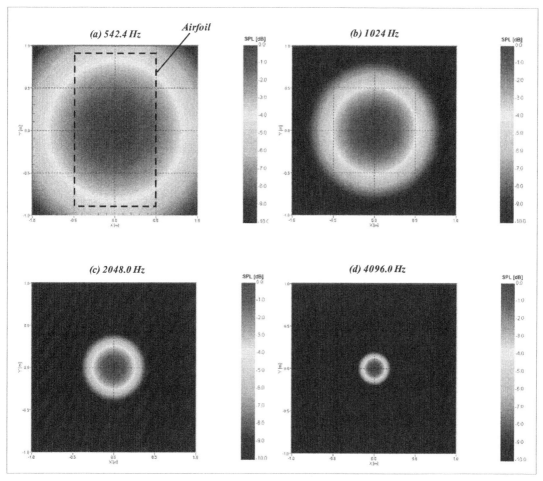

Figure 22. Star-array point-spread function for one-twelfth octave bands with center frequencies at (a) 542.4 Hz, (b) 1024.0 Hz, (c) 2048.0 Hz, and (d) 4096.0 Hz at a distance of 3.0 m (flow in the tunnel section is not accounted for in these results)

Phased-array data were acquired using a 64-Channel Agilent Data Acquisition System. The raw data consists of the time series of the 63 array microphones for each run. Fifty records, each of 16,384 points, were acquired from each microphone. A sampling frequency of 51,200 Hz was used. Acoustic maps were generated using a conventional frequency domain beamforming algorithm with diagonal removal. The algorithm incorporates the convective effect of the flow in the test section and the flow velocity discontinuity between the test section and the anechoic chamber. This algorithm has been used in previous experiments at Virginia Tech (Remillieux et al. 2007).

The equal-aperture spiral array was installed in the starboard-side chamber for the cases measured during the July entry. The star array was used in the second tunnel entry and installed in the port-side chamber. Figure 23 and Figure 24 show the position of the spiral and star arrays relative to the model, respectively. In all cases, the array was positioned 3 m away from the models.

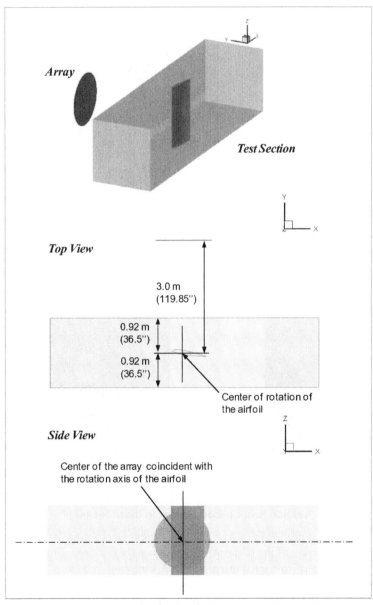

Figure 23. Position of the equal-aperture spiral array position on the starboard-side used during the July entry

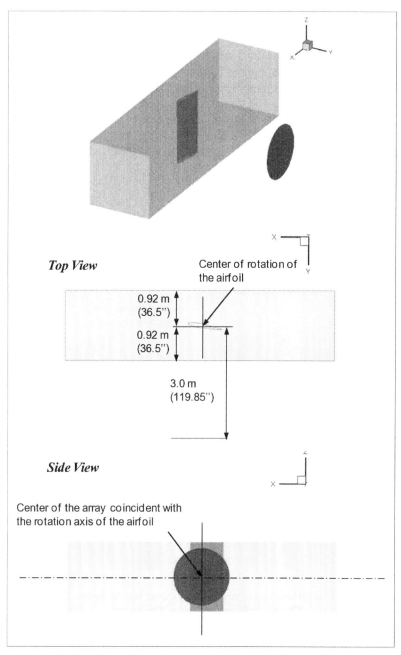

Top View

Center of rotation of the airfoil

0.92 m
(36.5'')

0.92 m
(36.5'')

3.0 m
(119.85'')

Side View

Center of the array coincident with
the rotation axis of the airfoil

Figure 24. Position of the star array on the port side used during the November-December entry

3. Aerodynamic Results and Discussions

Figure 25 shows the coordinate systems used in presenting the results of the airfoil tests. The chord-aligned airfoil system (x, y) has its origin at the leading edge of the airfoil, that origin moving with the leading edge as the angle of attack (α) is varied. This system is used to present mean-pressure distributions measured on the airfoil and to define the locations of the trailing-edge boundary-layer measurements. The tunnel fixed system (X, Y, Z) has its origin at the mid-span of the leading edge when the airfoil is at $0°$ angle of attack. This system is used for the wake and phased-array measurements. In terms of physical orientation in the wind tunnel, the view shown in Figure 25 is that seen looking downward along the airfoil span, and the starboard-side chamber appears at the top of the diagram.

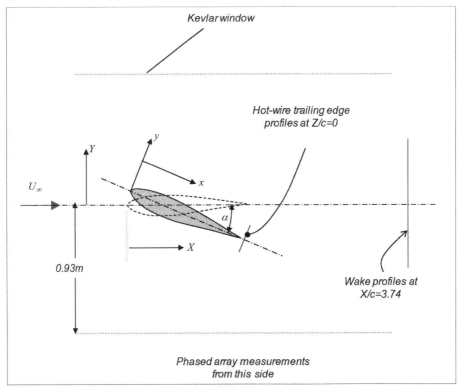

Figure 25. Measurement locations and coordinate systems for the tests; Z coordinate measured from center-span out of the paper

As discussed below, the effective angle of attack origin was determined through measurements of the airfoil pressure distributions. The origin of the geometric angle of attack was arbitrarily defined to be the same as that of the effective angle of attack (α_g and α_e both are 0 at the same airfoil position). This means that, for a cambered airfoil, a geometric angle of attack of 0 will not correspond to the position where the airfoil chord line is aligned with the test-section axis. Additionally, due to the interference correction, a variation of $1°$ in the geometric angle of attack results in a $0.78°$ change in effective angle of attack.

It is important to remember that the results presented below were measured as part of two tunnel entries and separated by four months. These tunnel entries used different airfoil-mounting arrangements and were separated by the complete dismantling and reassembly of the anechoic test section and chamber systems. As needed, this report indicates measurement dates and, thus, which tunnel entry these measurements were part of (either July 2007 or November-December 2007). For the most part, data from the two entries appears satisfyingly consistent. Where there are differences, they are pointed out and discussed as the data are presented. Measurements made during the July tunnel entry were carried out simultaneously with the calibration and understanding of the acoustic test section and its aerodynamic properties, and represent results from the first use of much of the hardware described above. In many cases, better understanding derived from a test yielded more-accurate estimates of the test conditions and any subsequent correction of the measurements. Although these final conditions do not fit as neatly into a test matrix, for the most part they do cover the same range of conditions originally intended.

3.1. Mean Pressure Distributions

Table 3 to Table 6 list the cases for which the mean pressure distributions were measured with each of the 4 airfoils. Most measurements were made at nominal Reynolds numbers of approximately 1,500,000 and 3,000,000, with angles of attack varying from zero lift to stall. In many cases, measurements were made both with and without boundary-layer trips.

Table 3. Test Matrix for the NACA 0012 Surface-Pressure Measurements

Date of Measurement	Geometric AoA α_g, deg.	Effective AoA, α_e, deg.	Chord Re	Trip	C_l	C_m	Data File
7/3/2007	0	0	1030000	No trip	-0.011	0.004	0012A
7/3/2007	0	0	1450000	No trip	-0.007	0.001	0012A
7/2/2007	0.5	0.4	1490000	No trip	0.03	0.001	0012A
7/3/2007	10.4	8.1	1480000	No trip	0.947	-0.012	0012A
7/3/2007	10.4	8.1	1520000	No trip	0.982	-0.018	0012A
7/3/2007	0	0	3070000	No trip	-0.012	0	0012A

Table 4. Test Matrix for the B1-18 Surface-Pressure Measurements

Date of Measurement	Geometric AoA, α_g, deg.	Effective AoA, α_e, deg.	Chord Re	Trip	C_l	C_m	Data File
11/28/2007	-2.6	-2	1570000	No trip	0.247	-0.116	B118Cp
11/28/2007	-2.1	-1.6	1600000	No trip	0.271	-0.108	B118Cp
7/13/2007	3.7	2.9	1510000	No trip	0.864	-0.132	B118A
11/28/2007	4.3	3.3	1550000	No trip	1.017	-0.128	B118Cp
7/13/2007	7.4	5.8	1550000	No trip	1.244	-0.135	B118A
11/28/2007	14.2	11	1640000	No trip	1.333	-0.153	B118Cp
7/13/2007	14.8	11.5	1540000	No trip	1.665	-0.138	B118A
11/28/2007	-6	-4.7	3200000	No trip	-0.157	-0.096	B118Cp
11/28/2007	-5.2	-4	3190000	No trip	-0.075	-0.099	B118Cp
7/24/2007	-4.4	-3.5	2980000	No trip	0.026	-0.111	B118D
7/23/2007	-3.6	-2.8	3090000	No trip	0.098	-0.112	B118D
7/23/2007	3.5	2.7	2940000	No trip	0.901	-0.132	B118D
11/28/2007	3.9	3	3200000	No trip	0.869	-0.125	B118Cp
7/21/2007	4.3	3.3	2940000	No trip	0.901	-0.132	B118B

Date of Measurement	Geometric AoA, α_g, deg.	Effective AoA, α_e, deg.	Chord Re	Trip	C_l	C_m	Data File
7/21/2007	6.2	4.8	2900000	No trip	1.114	-0.138	B118B
11/28/2007	7.7	6	3170000	No trip	1.273	-0.13	B118Cp
11/28/2007	14.2	11	3110000	No trip	1.765	-0.12	B118Cp
11/28/2007	16.7	13	3200000	No trip	1.394	-0.165	B118Cp
7/16/2007	7.4	5.8	1500000	Serrated tape	1.195	-0.129	B118A
7/21/2007	-3.8	-3	3130000	Serrated tape	0.126	-0.108	B118C
7/20/2007	-1.7	-1.3	3020000	Serrated tape	0.403	-0.132	B118B
7/20/2007	2.5	1.9	3000000	Serrated tape	0.768	-0.122	B118B
7/23/2007	4.9	3.8	3040000	Serrated tape	0.952	-0.129	B118C
7/21/2007	7.5	5.8	2920000	Serrated tape	1.312	-0.14	B118B
11/28/2007	7.7	6	3250000	Serrated tape	1.231	-0.127	B118Cp
7/24/2007	6.9	5.4	3030000	Soiled trip			B118D

Table 5. Test Matrix for the DU96 Surface-Pressure Measurements

Date of Measurement	Geometric AoA, α_g, deg.	Effective AoA, α_e, deg.	Chord Re	Trip	C_l	C_m	Data File
7/16/2007	-5.3	-4.1	1560000	No trip	-0.148	-0.04	DU96A
11/30/2007	-1.2	-0.9	1610000	No trip	0.182	-0.047	DU96Cp
11/30/2007	1.3	1	1600000	No trip	0.402	-0.054	DU96Cp
7/16/2007	3.9	3.1	1540000	No trip	0.628	-0.052	DU96A
11/30/2007	3.8	3	1580000	No trip	0.676	-0.061	DU96Cp
7/16/2007	9.2	7.2	1530000	No trip	1.061	-0.062	DU96A
11/30/2007	10.3	8	1610000	No trip	1.165	-0.064	DU96Cp
7/16/2007	13.1	10.2	1530000	No trip	1.228	-0.086	DU96A
11/30/2007	15.4	12	1570000	No trip	1.084	-0.066	DU96Cp
11/30/2007	15.4	12	1590000	No trip	1.087	-0.066	DU96Cp
7/19/2007	-5.3	-4.1	2840000	No trip	-0.126	-0.032	DU96B
7/19/2007	3.9	3.1	2850000	No trip	0.578	-0.049	DU96B
7/20/2007	7.9	6.1	2930000	No trip	0.994	-0.067	DU96B
11/30/2007	10.3	8	3190000	No trip	1.072	-0.074	DU96Cp
7/19/2007	13.1	10.2	2850000	No trip	1.215	-0.075	DU96B
11/30/2007	15.4	12	3150000	No trip	1.18	-0.083	DU96Cp
7/18/2007	8.5	6.7	1500000	Serrated tape	0.951	-0.051	DU96B
7/19/2007	9.2	7.2	2860000	Serrated tape	1.078	-0.075	DU96B
7/26/2007	9	7	2870000	Soiled trip			DU96C

Table 6. Test Matrix for the S831 Surface-Pressure Measurements

Date of Measurement	Geometric AoA, α_g, deg.	Effective AoA, α_e, deg.	Chord Re	Trip	C_l	C_m	Data File
7/10/2007	-9.1	-7.1	1510000	No trip	-0.176	-0.119	S831A1
7/12/2007	-9.1	-7.1	1500000	No trip	-0.053	-0.119	S831B
12/3/2007	-5.7	-4.5	1620000	No trip	0.342	-0.171	S831Cp
7/12/2007	-2.6	-2	1570000	No trip	0.471	-0.115	S831B
7/10/2007	-1.1	-0.9	1480000	No trip	0.619	-0.136	S831A1
12/3/2007	5.6	4.4	1620000	No trip	1.106	-0.154	S831Cp

Date of Measurement	Geometric AoA, α_g, deg.	Effective AoA, α_e, deg.	Chord Re	Trip	C_l	C_m	Data File
7/10/2007	6.5	5.1	1490000	No trip	1.155	-0.141	S831A1
7/12/2007	7.6	5.9	1510000	No trip	1.131	-0.125	S831B
7/25/2007	-9.6	-7.5	3060000	No trip	-0.102	-0.131	S831C
7/12/2007	-9.1	-7.1	3060000	No trip	-0.102	-0.131	S831B
7/25/2007	-2.2	-1.7	3050000	No trip	0.506	-0.13	S831C
12/3/2007	5.6	4.4	3190000	No trip	1.256	-0.162	S831Cp
12/3/2007	6.4	5	3150000	No trip	1.327	-0.166	S831Cp
7/25/2007	8.2	6.4	2980000	No trip	1.358	-0.164	S831C
12/3/2007	9.8	7.6	3130000	No trip	1.405	-0.157	S831Cp
7/24/2007	8.2	6.4	3020000	Serrated tape	1.226	-0.135	S831C
7/26/2007	8.2	6.4	3100000	Soiled trip	1.206	-0.135	S831C

The angle of attack origin of each airfoil was determined aerodynamically. After installing the airfoil, it was placed approximately (by eye) at zero angle of attack. A trial pressure distribution then was measured at a Reynolds number of approximately 3,000,000. The measured mean pressure distribution then was compared to a panel-method solution for the airfoil that assumed free-flight conditions to establish the actual effective angle of attack. The geometric angle of attack was determined using the 22% interference correction from Section 2. After the test matrix of pressure measurements was completed, this selection of the geometric angle of attack was reassessed by comparing the measured pressure distributions under all conditions with the panel-method solution.

The panel method described here is a standard linear-vortex panel method, similar to that described by Kuethe and Chow (1986). The method fixes the overall circulation by enforcing Kutta condition at the trailing edge. About 200 panels were used to represent the design shapes of the airfoils. The method included no means to model the splitter plate or its effects. The uncertainty in the zero value of the geometric angle of attack that is determined by comparison with the panel method is estimated to be $\pm 0.3°$.

Measured pressure distributions are plotted in Figure 26 to Figure 93 in terms of both chordwise distance (x/c) and edge-length (s/c—defined as the distance along the airfoil surface) measured from the trailing edge in the clockwise direction (defined in Figure 94). Plotting against s/c reveals details of the pressure distribution around the leading edge. Edge length is determined from chordwise position of the pressure taps using theoretical airfoil shapes. Pressures are plotted in terms of the following coefficient.

$$C_p = \frac{p - p_\infty}{p_{0\infty} - p_\infty} = \frac{p - p_\infty}{\frac{1}{2}\rho U_\infty^2}$$

Where p is the local pressure, $p_{0\infty}$ and p_∞ are the reference free-stream stagnation and static pressures, and U_∞ is the free-stream velocity.

The measured pressure distributions were integrated to estimate the lift and moment coefficients. To do this, the distributions first were interpolated in terms of edge length to 200 points distributed around the airfoil contour. To improve the accuracy of the interpolation around the stagnation region, a single data point of unit pressure coefficient at the theoretically determined stagnation location was added to the experimental data. The coefficients are plotted against effective angle of attack in Figure 95 through Figure 102 and are listed in Table 3 through Table 6. The lift coefficient plots include comparison with panel-method predictions. The overall lift and moment were not estimated for the cases where a soiled trip was used, because the trip covered too many of the pressure ports in the leading-edge region for such estimates to be accurate.

The pressure distributions for the NACA 0012 airfoil (Figure 26 to Figure 31) conform to the expectations of the panel-method predictions and largely confirm the free-flight behavior of this airfoil in the acoustic test section. The 3 pressure distributions measured at 0° angle of attack (Figure 26 to Figure 28) show little discernable influence of Reynolds number over a 3:1 range. The effects of a small angle of attack change can be discerned clearly in the pressure distribution measured at 0.5° effective angle of attack (Figure 29), the small difference between the upper and lower pressure distributions accurately tracks the panel-method solution in this case. The measurements at greater angle of attack (Figure 30, Figure 31) appear to confirm the interference correction of -22%, the pressure distributions measured at 10.4° geometric angle of attack fall very close to those predicted for an effective angle of attack of 8.1°, particularly over the forward part of the airfoil. In the trailing-edge region, measured pressures are slightly less than those predicted, perhaps as a result of the acceleration of the flow in this (almost) closed test section, as discussed above in Section 2. Good agreement between measurement and prediction also is seen in the integrated lift coefficients (Figure 95).

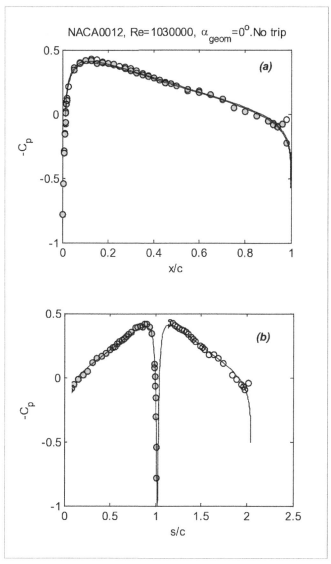

Figure 26. Mean pressure distribution on the NACA 0012 airfoil at 0° effective angle of attack and a Reynolds number of 1,030,000 without trip; filled symbols indicate suction side, open symbols indicate pressure side, dashed line indicates panel-method result; (a) pressure plotted versus chordwise distance (x/c), and (b) pressure plotted versus edge length (s/c)

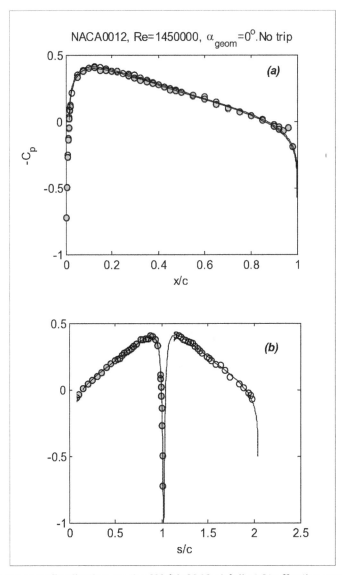

Figure 27. Mean pressure distribution on the NACA 0012 airfoil at 0° effective angle of attack and a Reynolds number of 1,450,000 without trip; filled symbols indicate suction side, open symbols indicate pressure side, dashed line indicates panel-method result; (a) pressure plotted versus chordwise distance (x/c), and (b) pressure plotted versus edge length (s/c)

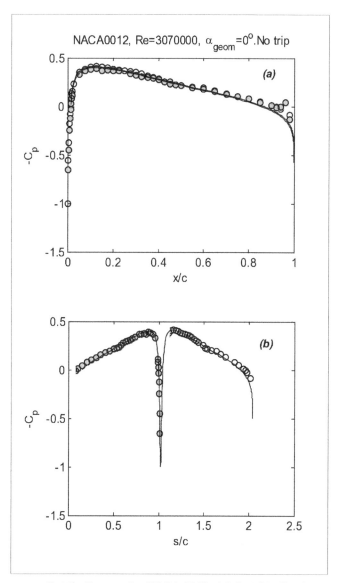

Figure 28. Mean pressure distribution on the NACA 0012 airfoil at 0° effective angle of attack and a Reynolds number of 3,070,000 without trip; filled symbols indicate suction side, open symbols pressure indicate side, dashed line indicates panel-method result; (a) pressure plotted versus chordwise distance (x/c), and (b) pressure plotted versus edge length (s/c)

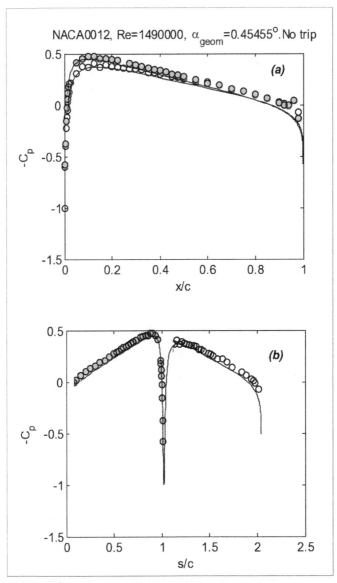

Figure 29. Mean pressure distribution on the NACA 0012 airfoil at 0.4° effective angle of attack and a Reynolds number of 1,490,000 without trip; filled symbols indicate suction side, open symbols indicate pressure side, dashed line indicates panel-method result; (a) pressure plotted versus chordwise distance (x/c), and (b) pressure plotted versus edge length (s/c)

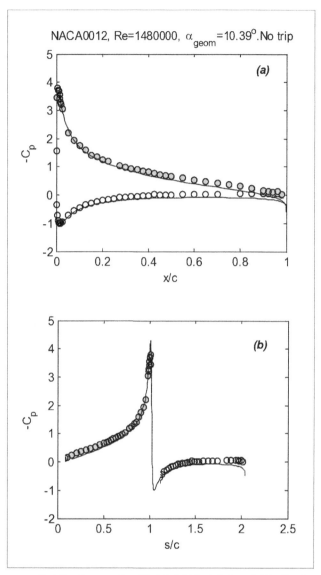

Figure 30. Mean pressure distribution on the NACA 0012 airfoil at 8.1° effective angle of attack and a Reynolds number of 1,480,000 without trip; filled symbols indicate suction side, open symbols indicate pressure side, dashed line indicates panel-method result; (a) pressure plotted versus chordwise distance (x/c), and (b) pressure plotted versus edge length (s/c)

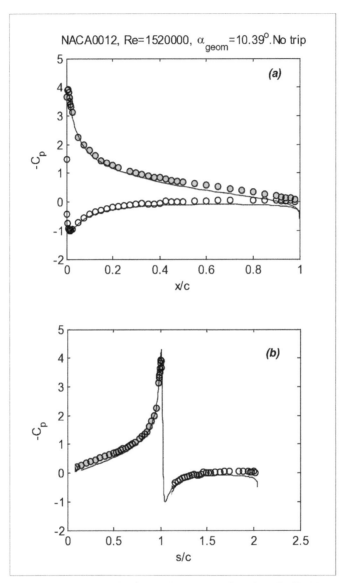

NACA0012, Re=1520000, α_{geom}=10.39°. No trip

Figure 31. Mean pressure distribution on the NACA 0012 airfoil at 8.1° effective angle of attack and a Reynolds number of 1,520,000 without trip; filled symbols indicate suction side, open symbols indicate pressure side, dashed line indicates panel-method result; (a) pressure plotted versus chordwise distance (x/c), and (b) pressure plotted versus edge length (s/c)

Pressure distributions for the B1-18 airfoil are organized by increasing angle of attack in Figure 32 to Figure 57. Corresponding lift and moment coefficient data are shown in Figure 97, Figure 98, and Table 4. Except at very low and very high angles of attack, the B1-18 airfoil appears to behave almost exactly as inviscid theory predicts. Measured lift coefficients and pressure distributions are close to those predicted using the panel method. Effects of Reynolds number and the serrated tape trip appear small (*c.f.* Figure 49 through Figure 53). For the one condition at which it was tested (Figure 48), the soiled trip appears to slightly increase the airfoil loading, but produces no qualitative change in the measured pressure distributions. At the largest effective negative angles of attack (Figure 32, Figure 33) the suction-side pressures fail to reach the peak negative values suggested by the panel method, resulting in an overall lift generated by the airfoil that is somewhat less than predicted. Indeed, the integrated lift results (Figure 97) show this to be part of a larger trend—the measured results deviate from inviscid expectations below about -2°. The researchers speculate that viscous flow effects in the leading-edge region might be responsible.

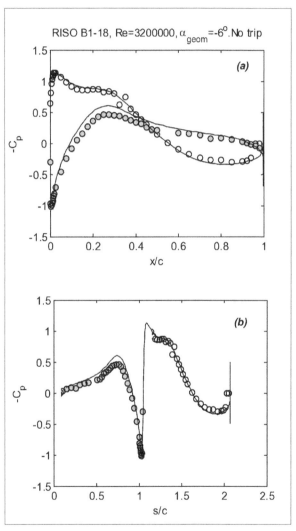

Figure 32. Mean pressure distribution on the B1-18 airfoil at -4.7° effective angle of attack and a Reynolds number of 3,200,000 without trip; filled symbols indicate suction side, open symbols indicate pressure side, dashed line indicates panel-method result; (a) pressure plotted versus chordwise distance (x/c), and (b) pressure plotted versus edge length (s/c)

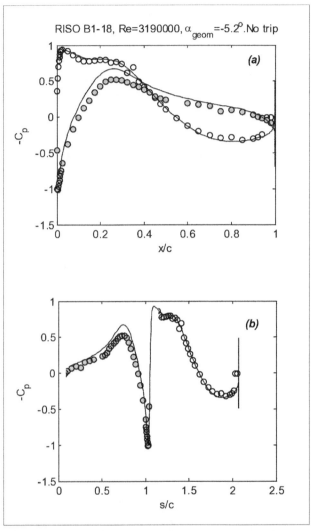

Figure 33. Mean pressure distribution on the B1-18 airfoil at -4° effective angle of attack and a Reynolds number of 3,200,000 without trip; filled symbols indicate suction side, open symbols indicate pressure side, dashed line indicates panel-method result; (a) pressure plotted versus chordwise distance (x/c), and (b) pressure plotted versus edge length (s/c)

At very high angles of attack, a more dramatic departure is observed as a result of separation of the flow from the suction surface. At the higher Reynolds number, the flow over the suction side appears almost completely attached at an 11° angle of attack (Figure 55), but is stalled almost completely at 13° (Figure 57). At the lower Reynolds number the behavior is more confusing, with the flow apparently stalled at 11° (Figure 54), but then partially attached at 11.5° (Figure 56). It is tempting to eliminate one or other of these results as some sort of experimental error. Careful re-examination of the experimental record, however, indicates that this is unlikely. Indeed, the low Reynolds number and high Reynolds number 11° results were measured as part of the same test run. Instead, researchers suspect that the low Reynolds number high angle of

43

attack flow over this airfoil might be sensitive to whether it is developing from a stalled or unstalled state as the tunnel is brought to test conditions. The 11° and 11.5° low Reynolds number measurements, could have been made at different stages of this stall behavior thus resulting in the difference. Such hysteresis in the stall behavior is a definite possibility given that they were obtained some 4 months apart as part of the 2 tunnel entries (*see* Table 4).

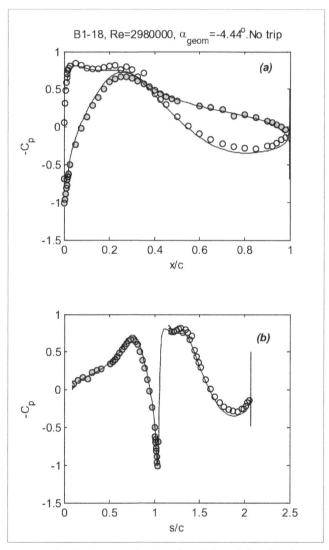

Figure 34. Mean pressure distribution on the B1-18 airfoil at -3.5° effective angle of attack and a Reynolds number of 2,980,000 without trip; filled symbols indicate suction side, open symbols indicate pressure side, dashed line indicates panel-method result; (a) pressure plotted versus chordwise distance (x/c), and (b) pressure plotted versus edge length (s/c)

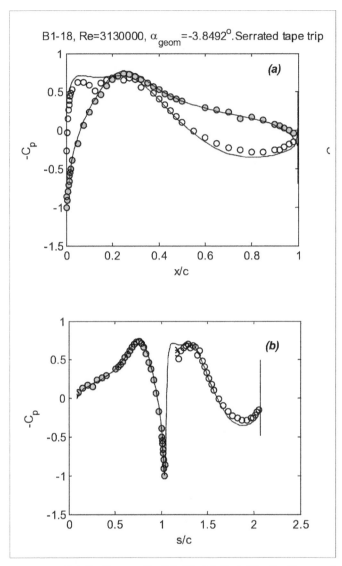

Figure 35. Mean pressure distribution on the B1-18 airfoil at -3° effective angle of attack and a Reynolds number of 3,130,000 with the serrated-tape trip; filled symbols indicate suction side, open symbols indicate pressure side, dashed line indicates panel-method result; (a) pressure plotted versus chordwise distance (x/c), and (b) pressure plotted versus edge length (s/c)

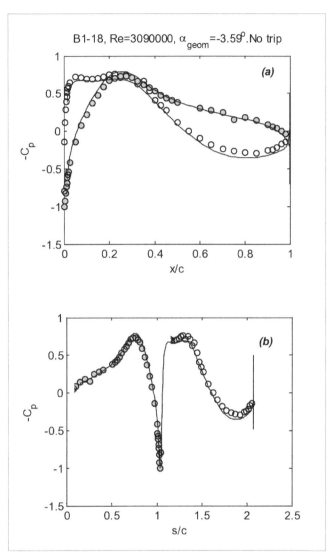

Figure 36. Mean pressure distribution on the B1-18 airfoil at -2.8° effective angle of attack and a Reynolds number of 3,090,000 without trip; filled symbols indicate suction side, open symbols indicate pressure side, dashed line indicates panel-method result; (a) pressure plotted versus chordwise distance (x/c), and (b) pressure plotted versus edge length (s/c)

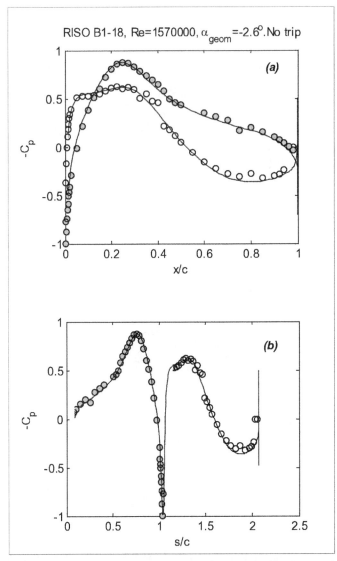

Figure 37. Mean pressure distribution on the B1-18 airfoil at -2° effective angle of attack and a Reynolds number of 1,570,000 without trip; filled symbols indicate suction side, open symbols indicate pressure side, dashed line indicates panel-method result; (a) pressure plotted versus chordwise distance (x/c), and (b) pressure plotted versus edge length (s/c)

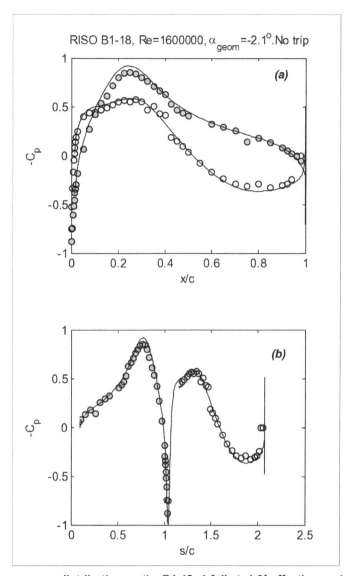

Figure 38. Mean pressure distribution on the B1-18 airfoil at -1.6° effective angle of attack and a Reynolds number of 1,600,000 without trip; filled symbols indicate suction side, open symbols indicate pressure side, dashed line indicates panel-method result; (a) pressure plotted versus chordwise distance (x/c), and (b) pressure plotted versus edge length (s/c)

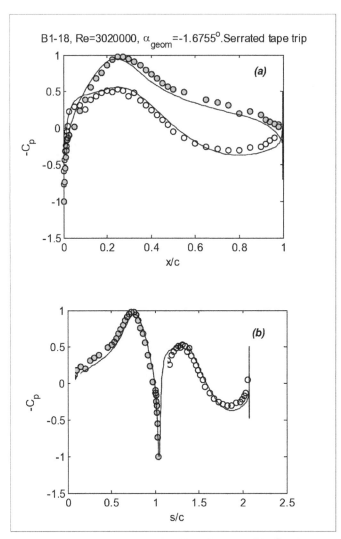

Figure 39. Mean pressure distribution on the B1-18 airfoil at -1.3° effective angle of attack and a Reynolds number of 3,020,000 with the serrated-tape trip; filled symbols indicate suction side, open symbols indicate pressure side, dashed line indicates panel-method result; (a) pressure plotted versus chordwise distance (x/c), and (b) pressure plotted versus edge length (s/c)

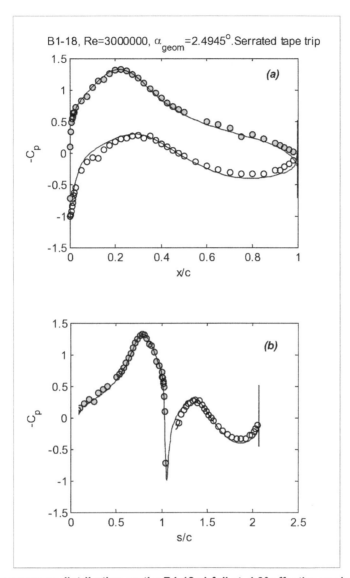

Figure 40. Mean pressure distribution on the B1-18 airfoil at -1.9° effective angle of attack and a Reynolds number of 3,000,000 with the serrated-tape trip; filled symbols indicate suction side, open symbols indicate pressure side, dashed line indicates panel-method result; (a) pressure plotted versus chordwise distance (x/c), and (b) pressure plotted versus edge length (s/c)

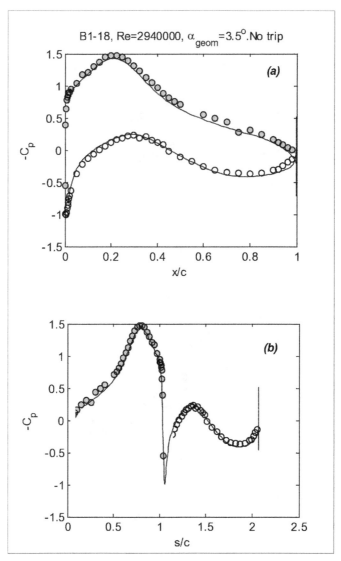

Figure 41. Mean pressure distribution on the B1-18 airfoil at 2.7° effective angle of attack and a Reynolds number of 2,940,000 without trip; filled symbols indicate suction side, open symbols indicate pressure side, dashed line indicates panel-method result; (a) pressure plotted versus chordwise distance (x/c), and (b) pressure plotted versus edge length (s/c)

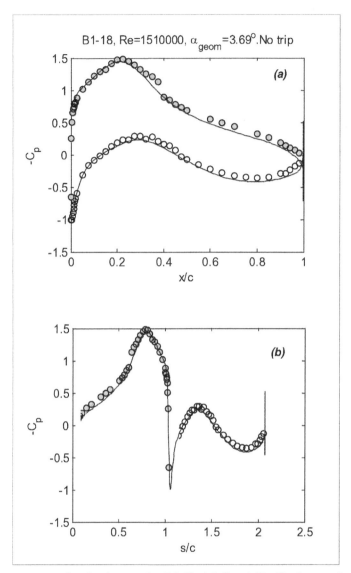

Figure 42. Mean pressure distribution on the B1-18 airfoil at 2.9° effective angle of attack and a Reynolds number of 1,510,000 without trip; filled symbols indicate suction side, open symbols indicate pressure side, dashed line indicates panel-method result; (a) pressure plotted versus chordwise distance (x/c), and (b) pressure plotted versus edge length (s/c)

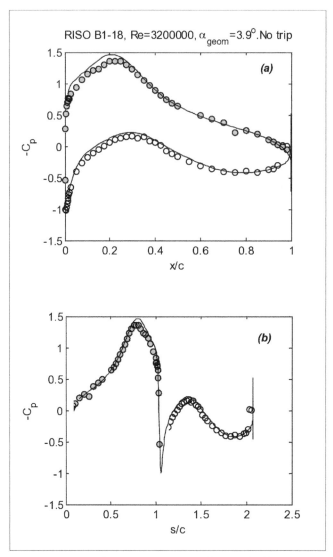

Figure 43. Mean pressure distribution on the B1-18 airfoil at 3° effective angle of attack and a Reynolds number of 3,200,000 without trip; filled symbols indicate suction side, open symbols indicate pressure side, dashed line indicates panel-method result; (a) pressure plotted versus chordwise distance (x/c), and (b) pressure plotted versus edge length (s/c)

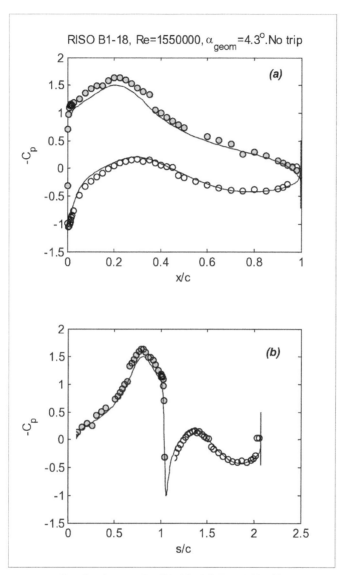

Figure 44. Mean pressure distribution on the B1-18 airfoil at 3.3° effective angle of attack and a Reynolds number of 1,550,000 without trip; filled symbols indicate suction side, open symbols indicate pressure side, dashed line indicates panel-method result; (a) pressure plotted versus chordwise distance (x/c), and (b) pressure plotted versus edge length (s/c)

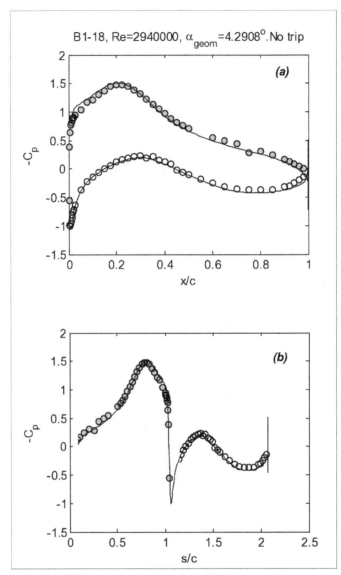

Figure 45. Mean pressure distribution on the B1-18 airfoil at 3.3° effective angle of attack and a Reynolds number of 2,940,000 without trip; filled symbols indicate suction side, open symbols indicate pressure side, dashed line indicates panel-method result; (a) pressure plotted versus chordwise distance (x/c), and (b) pressure plotted versus edge length (s/c)

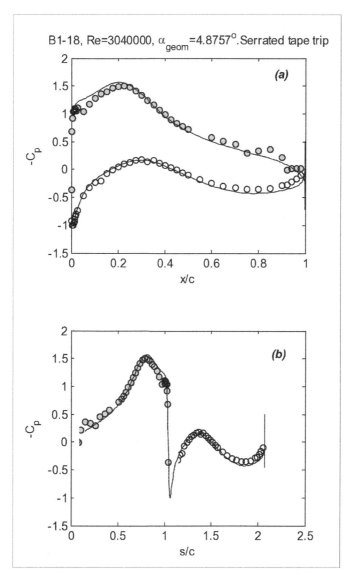

Figure 46. Mean pressure distribution on the B1-18 airfoil at 3.8° effective angle of attack and a Reynolds number of 3,040,000 with the serrated-tape trip; filled symbols indicate suction side, open symbols indicate pressure side, dashed line indicates panel-method result; (a) pressure plotted versus chordwise distance (x/c), and (b) pressure plotted versus edge length (s/c)

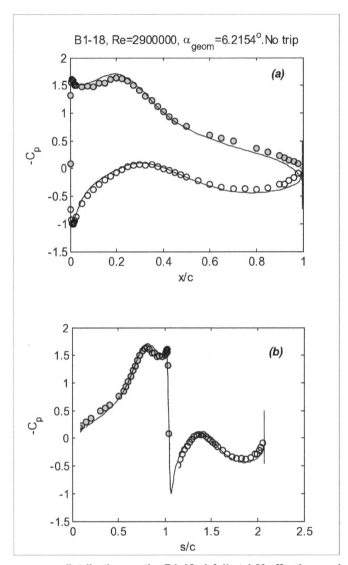

Figure 47. Mean pressure distribution on the B1-18 airfoil at 4.8° effective angle of attack and a Reynolds number of 2,900,000 without trip; filled symbols indicate suction side, open symbols indicate pressure side, dashed line indicates panel-method result; (a) pressure plotted versus chordwise distance (x/c), and (b) pressure plotted versus edge length (s/c)

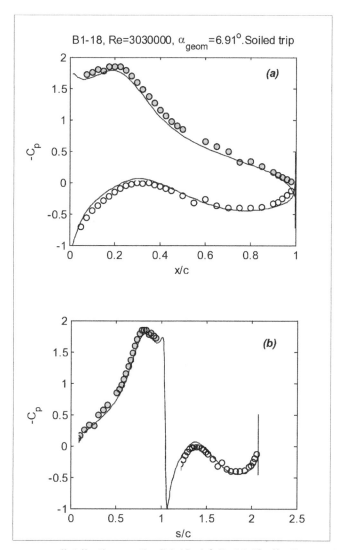

Figure 48. Mean pressure distribution on the B1-18 airfoil at 5.4° effective angle of attack and a Reynolds number of 3,030,000 with the soiled trip; filled symbols indicate suction side, open symbols indicate pressure side, dashed line indicates panel-method result; (a) pressure plotted versus chordwise distance (x/c), and (b) pressure plotted versus edge length (s/c)

58

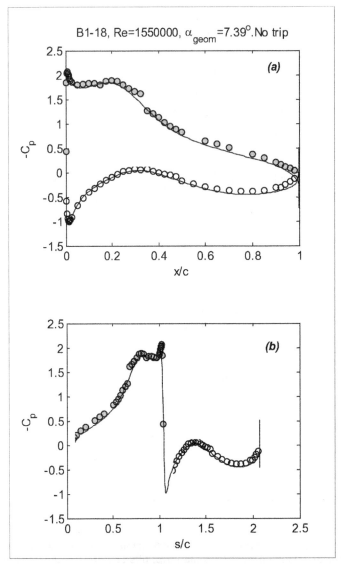

Figure 49. Mean pressure distribution on the B1-18 airfoil at 5.8° effective angle of attack and a Reynolds number of 1,550,000 without trip; filled symbols indicate suction side, open symbols indicate pressure side, dashed line indicates panel-method result; (a) pressure plotted versus chordwise distance (x/c), and (b) pressure plotted versus edge length (s/c)

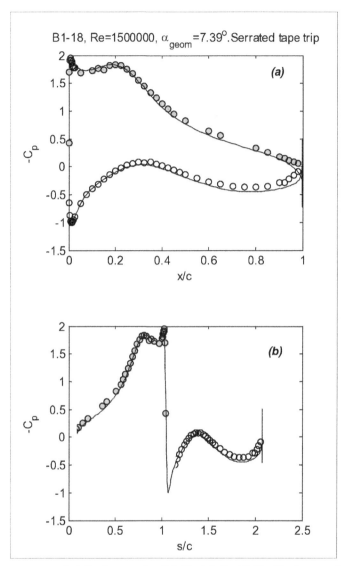

Figure 50. Mean pressure distribution on the B1-18 airfoil at 5.8° effective angle of attack and a Reynolds number of 1,500,000 with the serrated-tape trip; filled symbols indicate suction side, open symbols indicate pressure side, dashed line indicates panel-method result; (a) pressure plotted versus chordwise distance (x/c), and (b) pressure plotted versus edge length (s/c)

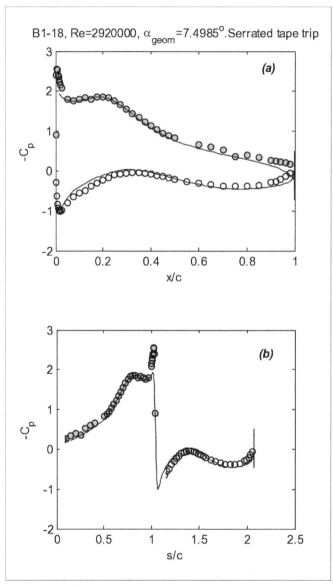

Figure 51. Mean pressure distribution on the B1-18 airfoil at 5.8° effective angle of attack and a Reynolds number of 2,920,000 without trip; filled symbols indicate suction side, open symbols indicate pressure side, dashed line indicates panel-method result; (a) pressure plotted versus chordwise distance (x/c), and (b) pressure plotted versus edge length (s/c)

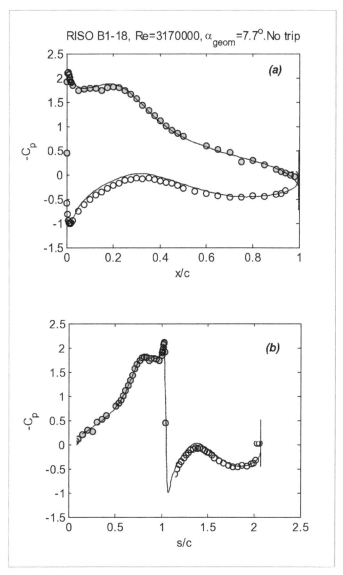

Figure 52. Mean pressure distribution on the B1-18 airfoil at 6° effective angle of attack and a Reynolds number of 3,170,000 without trip; filled symbols indicate suction side, open symbols indicate pressure side, dashed line indicates panel-method result; (a) pressure plotted versus chordwise distance (x/c), and (b) pressure plotted versus edge length (s/c)

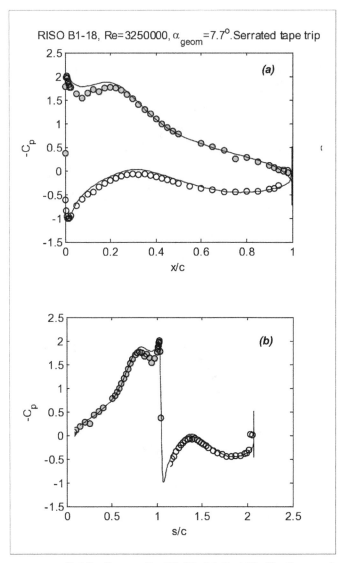

Figure 53. Mean pressure distribution on the B1-18 airfoil at 6° effective angle of attack and a Reynolds number of 3,250,000 with the serrated-tape trip; filled symbols indicate suction side, open symbols indicate pressure side, dashed line indicates panel-method result; (a) pressure plotted versus chordwise distance (x/c), and (b) pressure plotted versus edge length (s/c)

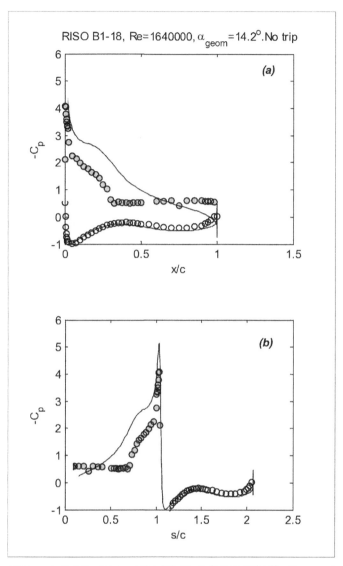

Figure 54. Mean pressure distribution on the B1-18 airfoil at 11° effective angle of attack and a Reynolds number of 1,640,000 without trip; filled symbols indicate suction side, open symbols indicate pressure side, dashed line indicates panel-method result; (a) pressure plotted versus chordwise distance (x/c), and (b) pressure plotted versus edge length (s/c)

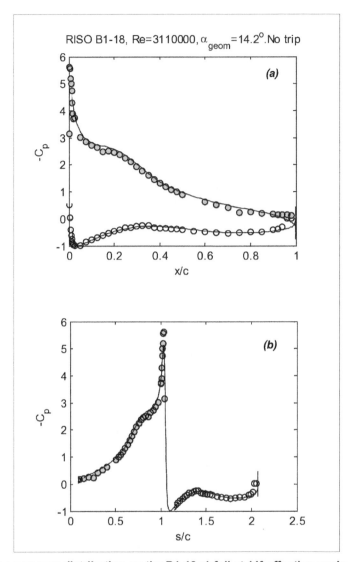

Figure 55. Mean pressure distribution on the B1-18 airfoil at 11° effective angle of attack and a Reynolds number of 3,110,000 without trip; filled symbols indicate suction side, open symbols indicate pressure side, dashed line indicates panel-method result; (a) pressure plotted versus chordwise distance (x/c), and (b) pressure plotted versus edge length (s/c)

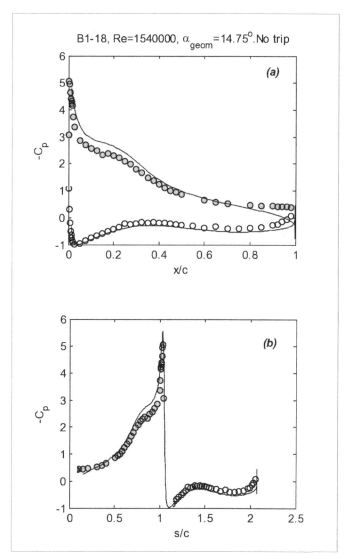

Figure 56. Mean pressure distribution on the B1-18 airfoil at 11.5° effective angle of attack and a Reynolds number of 1,540,000 without trip; filled symbols indicate suction side, open symbols indicate pressure side, dashed line indicates panel-method result; (a) pressure plotted versus chordwise distance (x/c), and (b) pressure plotted versus edge length (s/c)

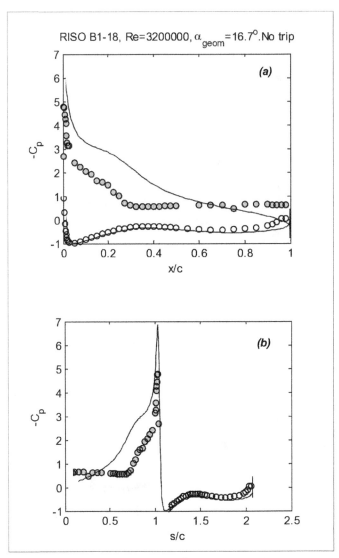

Figure 57. Mean pressure distribution on the B1-18 airfoil at 13° effective angle of attack and a Reynolds number of 3,200,000 without trip; filled symbols indicate suction side, open symbols indicate pressure side, dashed line indicates panel-method result; (a) pressure plotted versus chordwise distance (x/c), and (b) pressure plotted versus edge length (s/c)

Integrated lift coefficient values for the DU96 airfoil (Figure 99) show close agreement with the inviscid results around the zero lift angle of attack (approximately -3°), that slowly worsens as the angle of attack is increased. Over much of the angle of attack range, measured lift coefficients are about 10% below those predicted by the panel method. The pressure distributions (Figure 58 to Figure 75) show that this difference primarily is due to the suction-side flow, particularly over the forward half of the airfoil. Figure 69 is a typical example. The inviscid pressure distribution inferred from the design shape is characterized by a plateau region in which the pressure remains almost constant from the leading-edge region until about the 30% or 40% location. Except at the lowest angles of attack, the predicted pressure distribution is consistently overestimating this low pressure region. The magnitude of the resulting difference increases with increasing angle of attack and appears continuous with the effects of stall. These become clearly visible as the angle of attack is increased to 10.2° and 12° (Figure 72 to Figure 75). The soiled trip has little qualitative or quantitative effect on the pressure distribution (*c.f.* Figure 67 and Figure 68), whereas the serrated-tape trip slightly worsens the agreement with the panel method (*see* Figure 68, Figure 69).

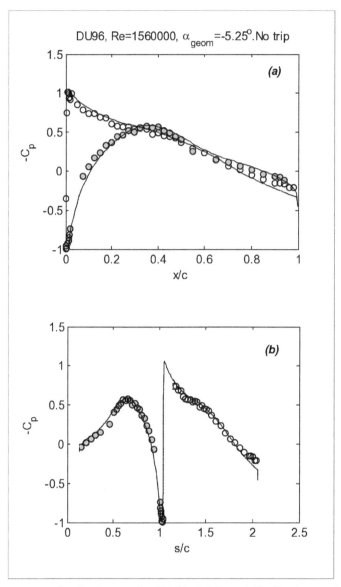

Figure 58. Mean pressure distribution on the DU-96 airfoil at -4.1° effective angle of attack and a Reynolds number of 1,560,000 without trip; filled symbols indicate suction side, open symbols indicate pressure side, dashed line indicates panel-method result; (a) pressure plotted versus chordwise distance (x/c), and (b) pressure plotted versus edge length (s/c)

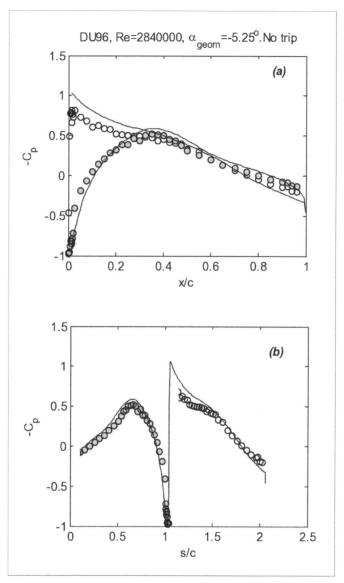

Figure 59. Mean pressure distribution on the DU-96 airfoil at -4.1° effective angle of attack and a Reynolds number of 2,840,000 without trip; filled symbols indicate suction side, open symbols indicate pressure side, dashed line indicates panel-method result; (a) pressure plotted versus chordwise distance (x/c), and (b) pressure plotted versus edge length (s/c)

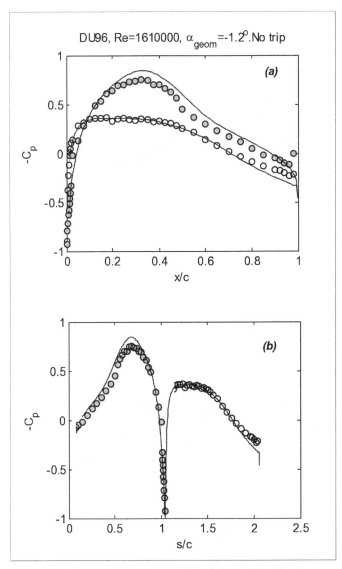

Figure 60. Mean pressure distribution on the DU-96 airfoil at -0.9° effective angle of attack and a Reynolds number of 1,610,000 without trip; filled symbols indicate suction side, open symbols indicate pressure side, dashed line indicates panel-method result; (a) pressure plotted versus chordwise distance (x/c), and (b) pressure plotted versus edge length (s/c)

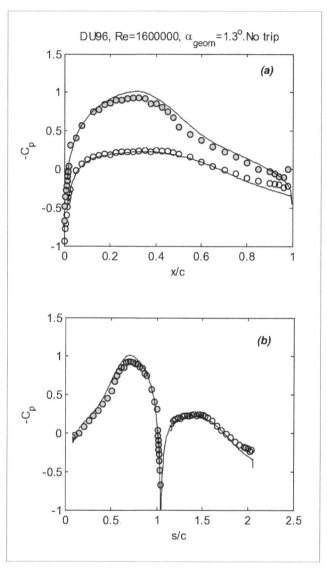

Figure 61. Mean pressure distribution on the DU-96 airfoil at 1° effective angle of attack and a Reynolds number of 1,600,000 without trip; filled symbols indicate suction side, open symbols indicate pressure side, dashed line indicates panel-method result; (a) pressure plotted versus chordwise distance (x/c), and (b) pressure plotted versus edge length (s/c)

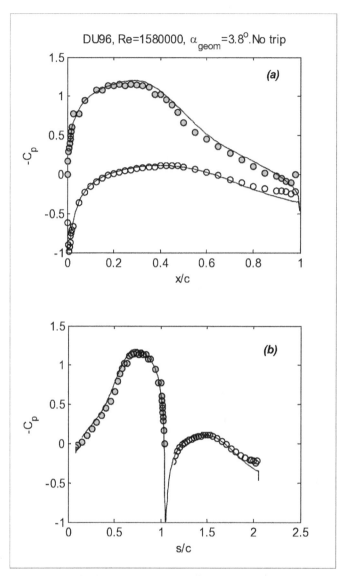

Figure 62. Mean pressure distribution on the DU-96 airfoil at 3° effective angle of attack and a Reynolds number of 1,580,000 without trip; filled symbols indicate suction side, open symbols indicate pressure side, dashed line indicates panel-method result; (a) pressure plotted versus chordwise distance (x/c), and (b) pressure plotted versus edge length (s/c)

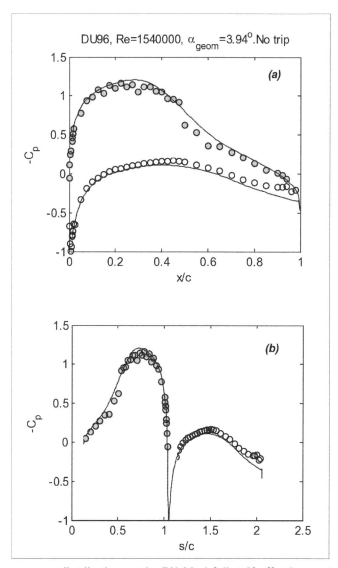

Figure 63. Mean pressure distribution on the DU-96 airfoil at 3° effective angle of attack and a Reynolds number of 1,540,000 without trip; filled symbols indicate suction side, open symbols indicate pressure side, dashed line indicates panel-method result; (a) pressure plotted versus chordwise distance (x/c), and (b) pressure plotted versus edge length (s/c)

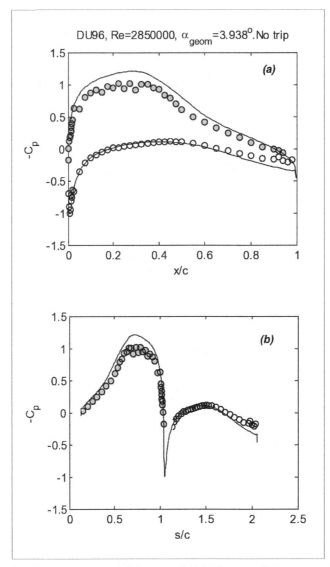

Figure 64. Mean pressure distribution on the DU-96 airfoil at 3° effective angle of attack and a Reynolds number of 2,850,000 without trip; filled symbols indicate suction side, open symbols indicate pressure side, dashed line indicates panel-method result; (a) pressure plotted versus chordwise distance (x/c), and (b) pressure plotted versus edge length (s/c)

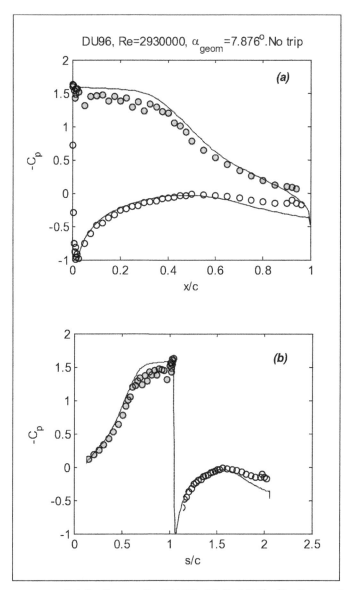

Figure 65. Mean pressure distribution on the DU-96 airfoil at 6.1° effective angle of attack and a Reynolds number of 2,930,000 without trip; filled symbols indicate suction side, open symbols indicate pressure side, dashed line indicates panel-method result; (a) pressure plotted versus chordwise distance (x/c), and (b) pressure plotted versus edge length (s/c)

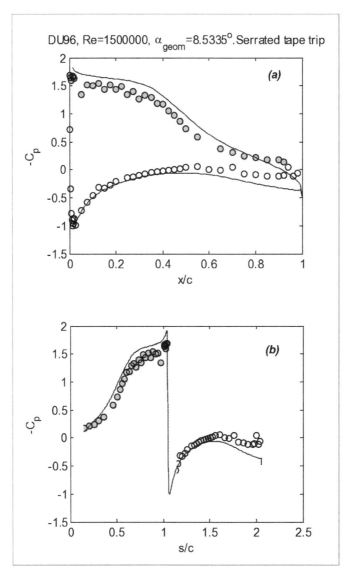

Figure 66. Mean pressure distribution on the DU-96 airfoil at 6.7° effective angle of attack and a Reynolds number of 1,500,000 with the serrated-tape trip; filled symbols indicate suction side, open symbols indicate pressure side, dashed line indicates panel-method result; (a) pressure plotted versus chordwise distance (x/c), and (b) pressure plotted versus edge length (s/c)

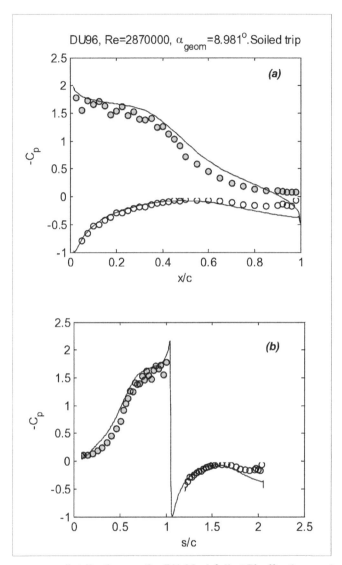

Figure 67. Mean pressure distribution on the DU-96 airfoil at 7° effective angle of attack and a Reynolds number of 2,870,000 with the soiled trip; filled symbols indicate suction side, open symbols indicate pressure side, dashed line indicates panel-method result; (a) pressure plotted versus chordwise distance (x/c), and (b) pressure plotted versus edge length (s/c)

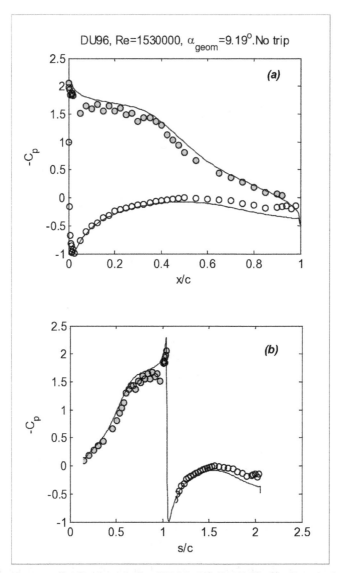

Figure 68. Mean pressure distribution on the DU-96 airfoil at 7.2° effective angle of attack and a Reynolds number of 1,530,000 without trip; filled symbols indicate suction side, open symbols indicate pressure side, dashed line indicates panel-method result; (a) pressure plotted versus chordwise distance (x/c), and (b) pressure plotted versus edge length (s/c)

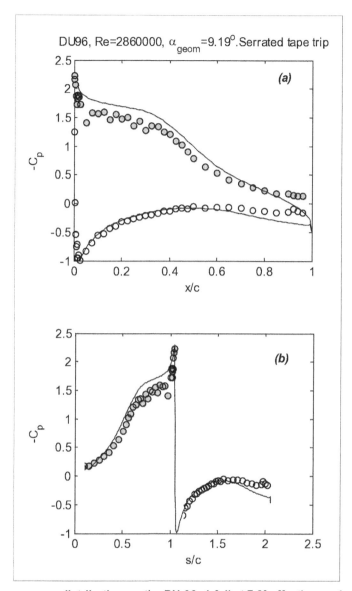

Figure 69. Mean pressure distribution on the DU-96 airfoil at 7.2° effective angle of attack and a Reynolds number of 2,860,000 with the serrated-tape trip; filled symbols indicate suction side, open symbols indicate pressure side, dashed line indicates panel-method result; (a) pressure plotted versus chordwise distance (x/c), and (b) pressure plotted versus edge length (s/c)

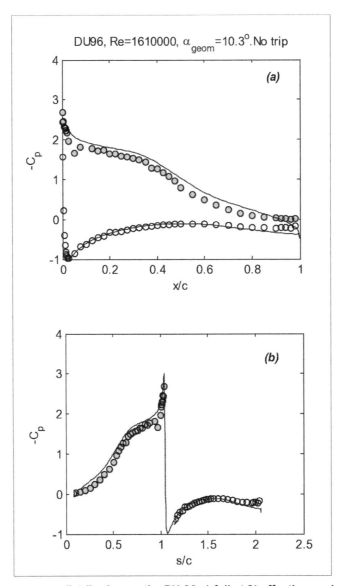

Figure 70. Mean pressure distribution on the DU-96 airfoil at 8° effective angle of attack and a Reynolds number of 1,610,000 without trip; filled symbols indicate suction side, open symbols indicate pressure side, dashed line indicates panel-method result; (a) pressure plotted versus chordwise distance (x/c), and (b) pressure plotted versus edge length (s/c)

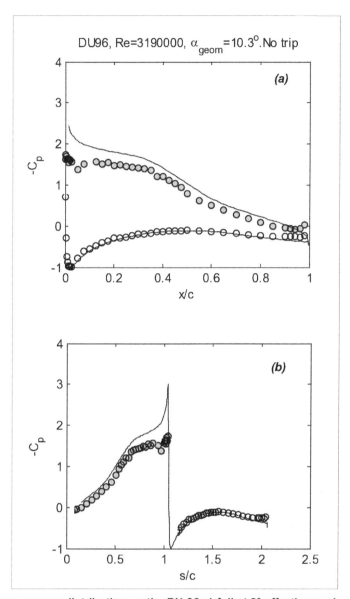

Figure 71. Mean pressure distribution on the DU-96 airfoil at 8° effective angle of attack and a Reynolds number of 3,190,000 without trip; filled symbols indicate suction side, open symbols indicate pressure side, dashed line indicates panel-method result; (a) pressure plotted versus chordwise distance (x/c), and (b) pressure plotted versus edge length (s/c)

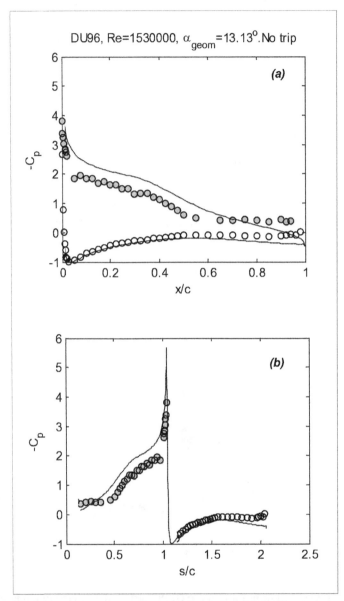

Figure 72. Mean pressure distribution on the DU-96 airfoil at 10.2° effective angle of attack and a Reynolds number of 1,530,000 without trip; filled symbols indicate suction side, open symbols indicate pressure side, dashed line indicates panel-method result; (a) pressure plotted versus chordwise distance (x/c), and (b) pressure plotted versus edge length (s/c)

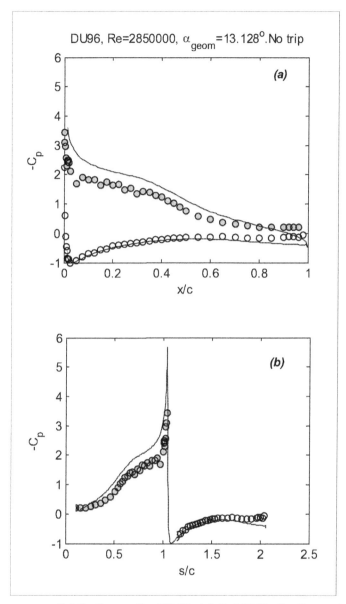

Figure 73. Mean pressure distribution on the DU-96 airfoil at 10.2° effective angle of attack and a Reynolds number of 2,850,000 without trip; filled symbols indicate suction side, open symbols indicate pressure side, dashed line indicates panel-method result; (a) pressure plotted versus chordwise distance (x/c), and (b) pressure plotted versus edge length (s/c)

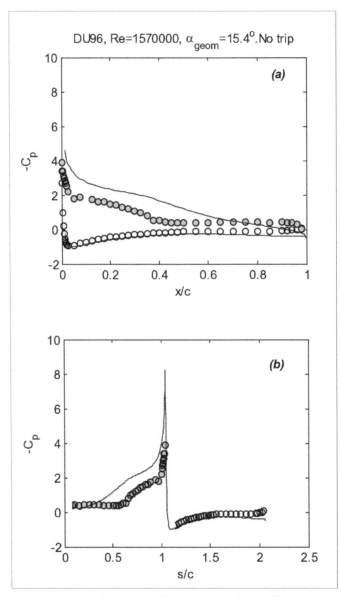

Figure 74. Mean pressure distribution on the DU-96 airfoil at 12° effective angle of attack and a Reynolds number of 1,570,000 without trip; filled symbols indicate suction side, open symbols indicate pressure side, dashed line indicates panel-method result; (a) pressure plotted versus chordwise distance (x/c), and (b) pressure plotted versus edge length (s/c)

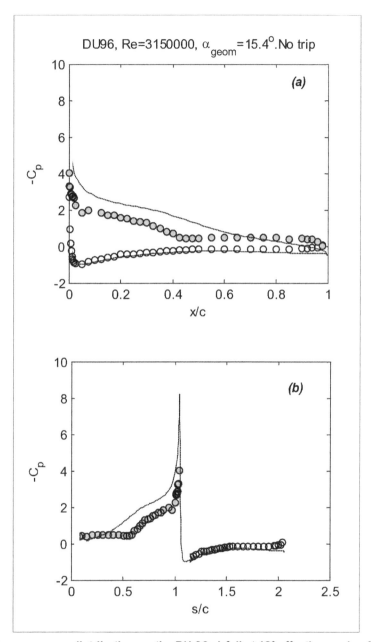

Figure 75. Mean pressure distribution on the DU-96 airfoil at 12° effective angle of attack and a Reynolds number of 3,150,000 without trip; filled symbols indicate suction side, open symbols indicate pressure side, dashed line indicates panel-method result; (a) pressure plotted versus chordwise distance (x/c), and (b) pressure plotted versus edge length (s/c)

The pressure measurements with the S831caused considerable upset in the test schedule of the first wind tunnel entry. This was the first airfoil tested after the NACA 0012, and immediately it was found that the pressure distribution—even at moderate angles of attack—did not correlate well with expectations based on the panel method. At that time, researchers had limited experience with the facility therefore much time was spent attempting to fix this "problem." Now, with the benefit of hindsight, the researchers realize that the airfoil itself was not performing well over a substantial portion of the test matrix. The measured pressure distributions (Figure 76 to Figure 93) show the best agreement with the panel method at near zero lift (close to -7°). At -7.5° and -7.1° the inviscid pressure distribution contains a sharp spike near the leading edge on the pressure side where, theoretically, the pressure coefficient falls below -7. This spike is associated with flow around the rather sharp leading edge of this airfoil from the suction-side stagnation point produced at this angle of attack. The flow would not be expected to actually achieve such a low pressure but instead to smooth this feature through a local thickening of the boundary layer or a region of local separation. Such a region of separation is visible in the low–Reynolds number measurements (*see* Figure 77, Figure 78). In particular, a region of near-constant pressure occupies the first 10% chord of the pressure-side pressure distribution. At high Reynolds numbers (Figure 76, Figure 79) the correlation with the panel method is much better, the signs of separation in the pressure distribution being much reduced. A good agreement with the inviscid calculation is also seen at -4.5° (Figure 80), but not at any greater angles of attack.

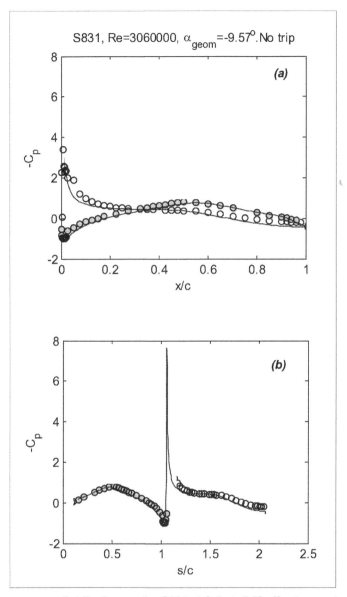

Figure 76. Mean pressure distribution on the S831 airfoil at -7.5° effective angle of attack and a Reynolds number of 3,060,000 without trip; filled symbols indicate suction side, open symbols indicate pressure side, dashed line indicates panel-method result; (a) pressure plotted versus chordwise distance (x/c), and (b) pressure plotted versus edge length (s/c)

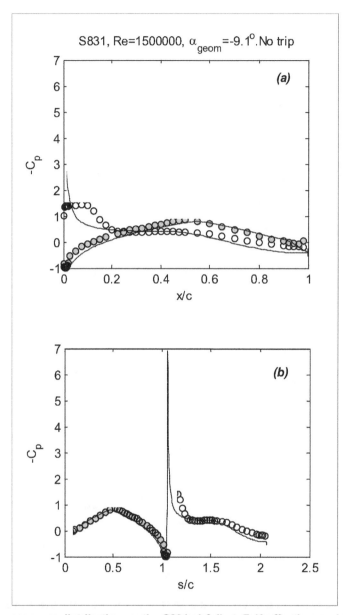

Figure 77. Mean pressure distribution on the S831 airfoil at -7.1° effective angle of attack and a Reynolds number of 1,500,000 without trip; filled symbols indicate suction side, open symbols indicate pressure side, dashed line indicates panel-method result; (a) pressure plotted versus chordwise distance (x/c), and (b) pressure plotted versus edge length (s/c)

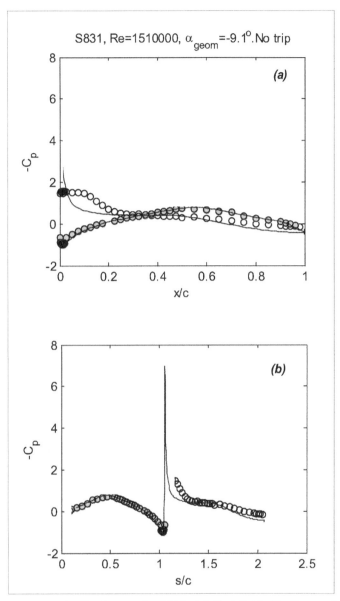

Figure 78. Mean pressure distribution on the S831 airfoil at -7.1° effective angle of attack and a Reynolds number of 1,510,000 without trip; filled symbols indicate suction side, open symbols indicate pressure side, dashed line indicates panel-method result; (a) pressure plotted versus chordwise distance (x/c), and (b) pressure plotted versus edge length (s/c)

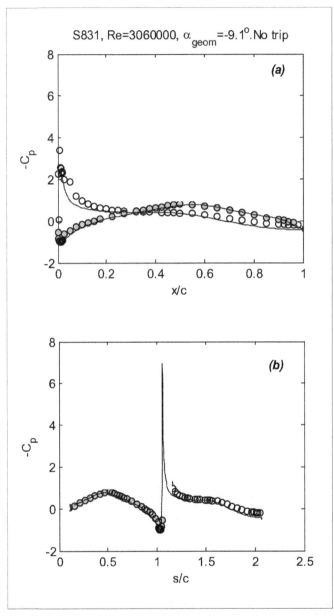

Figure 79. Mean pressure distribution on the S831 airfoil at -7.1° effective angle of attack and a Reynolds number of 3,060,000 without trip; filled symbols indicate suction side, open symbols indicate pressure side, dashed line indicates panel-method result; (a) pressure plotted versus chordwise distance (x/c), and (b) pressure plotted versus edge length (s/c)

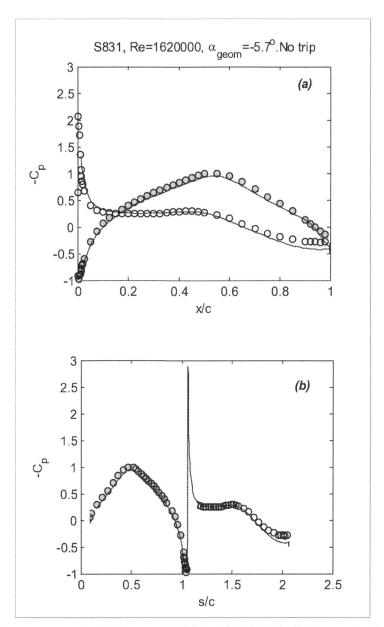

Figure 80. Mean pressure distribution on the S831 airfoil at -4.5° effective angle of attack and a Reynolds number of 1,620,000 without trip; filled symbols indicate suction side, open symbols indicate pressure side, dashed line indicates panel-method result; (a) pressure plotted versus chordwise distance (x/c), and (b) pressure plotted versus edge length (s/c)

Two different behaviors are seen relative to the panel-method predictions at larger angles of attack. The first—clearly seen in Figure 81, but visible in all the pressure distributions measured at angles of attack greater than -4.5°—is that the pressure distributions measured aft of mid-chord simply fail to follow the predictions; the difference between the pressures on the two sides of the airfoils being about half of that expected. Wake measurements (described below) and tuft flow visualizations showed this to be the result of a large three-dimensional region of separation located on the suction side downstream of mid-chord. The second behavior is seen for angles of attack greater than 4°. At approximately this angle of attack, the predicted suction-side pressure distribution (e.g., Figure 84) develops a distinct knee or peak in the leading-edge region that is followed by a region of almost constant pressure that occupies the forward half of the airfoil. At low Reynolds numbers the low pressures predicted for the constant-pressure region simply never are achieved, presumably because of viscous effects in the leading-edge region. At high Reynolds numbers, the flow does follow this behavior but only up to an angle of attack of 5°, beyond which the same discrepancy appears. Neither of the two trips seems to have much positive impact upon either of these behaviors (*c.f.* Figure 89 through Figure 91). At all angles of attack greater than -4.5°, the integrated lift coefficients fall well below those expected from the panel method (Figure 101).

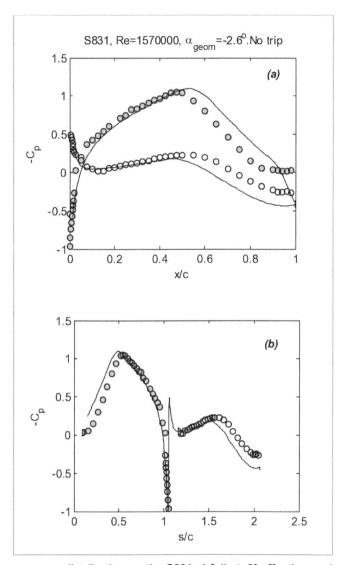

Figure 81. Mean pressure distribution on the S831 airfoil at -2° effective angle of attack and a Reynolds number of 1,570,000 without trip; filled symbols indicate suction side, open symbols indicate pressure side, dashed line indicates panel-method result; (a) pressure plotted versus chordwise distance (x/c), and (b) pressure plotted versus edge length (s/c)

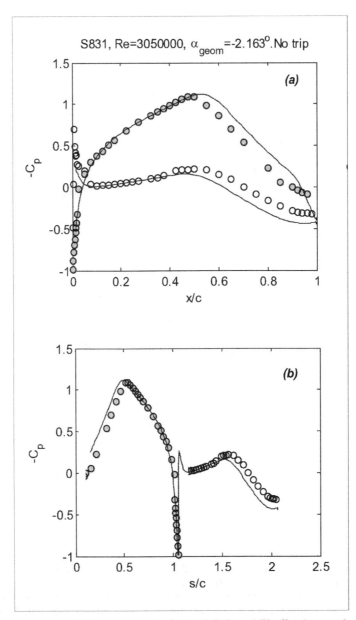

Figure 82. Mean pressure distribution on the S831 airfoil at -1.7° effective angle of attack and a Reynolds number of 3,050,000 without trip; filled symbols indicate suction side, open symbols indicate pressure side, dashed line indicates panel-method result; (a) pressure plotted versus chordwise distance (x/c), and (b) pressure plotted versus edge length (s/c)

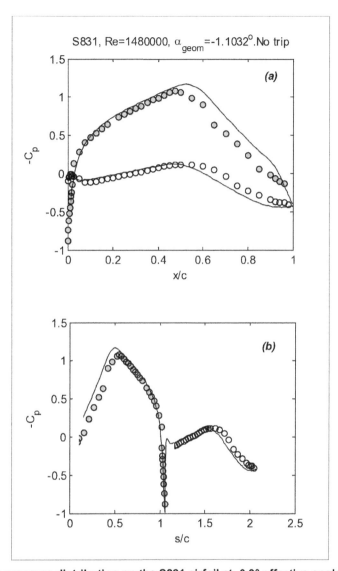

Figure 83. Mean pressure distribution on the S831 airfoil at -0.9° effective angle of attack and a Reynolds number of 1,480,000 without trip; filled symbols indicate suction side, open symbols indicate pressure side, dashed line indicates panel-method result; (a) pressure plotted versus chordwise distance (x/c), and (b) pressure plotted versus edge length (s/c)

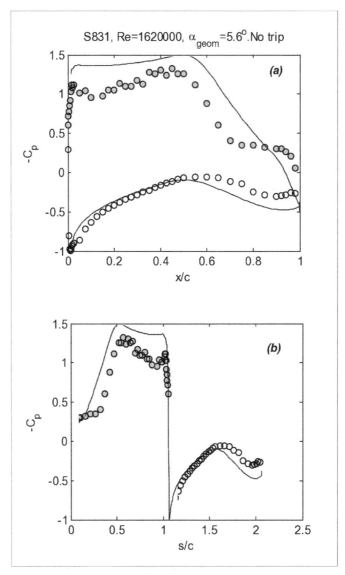

Figure 84. Mean pressure distribution on the S831 airfoil at 4.4° effective angle of attack and a Reynolds number of 1,620,000 without trip; filled symbols indicate suction side, open symbols indicate pressure side, dashed line indicates panel-method result; (a) pressure plotted versus chordwise distance (x/c), and (b) pressure plotted versus edge length (s/c)

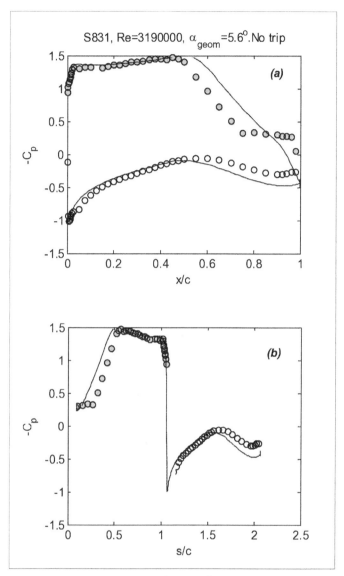

Figure 85. Mean pressure distribution on the S831 airfoil at 4.4° effective angle of attack and a Reynolds number of 3,190,000 without trip; filled symbols indicate suction side, open symbols indicate pressure side, dashed line indicates panel-method result; (a) pressure plotted versus chordwise distance (x/c), and (b) pressure plotted versus edge length (s/c)

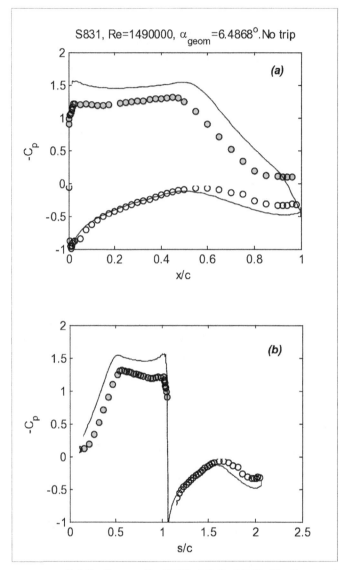

Figure 86. Mean pressure distribution on the S831 airfoil at 5.1° effective angle of attack and a Reynolds number of 1,490,000 without trip; filled symbols indicate suction side, open symbols indicate pressure side, dashed line indicates panel-method result; (a) pressure plotted versus chordwise distance (x/c), and (b) pressure plotted versus edge length (s/c)

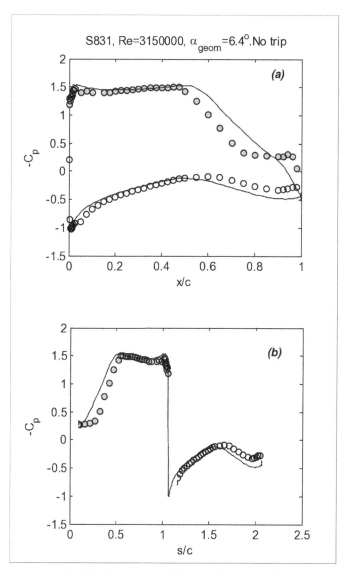

Figure 87. Mean pressure distribution on the S831 airfoil at 5.0° effective angle of attack and a Reynolds number of 3,150,000 without trip; filled symbols indicate suction side, open symbols indicate pressure side, dashed line indicates panel-method result; (a) pressure plotted versus chordwise distance (x/c), and (b) pressure plotted versus edge length (s/c)

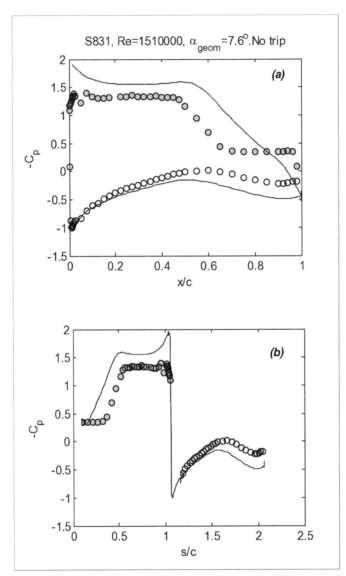

Figure 88. Mean pressure distribution on the S831 airfoil at 5.9° effective angle of attack and a Reynolds number of 1,510,000 without trip; filled symbols indicate suction side, open symbols indicate pressure side, dashed line indicates panel-method result; (a) pressure plotted versus chordwise distance (x/c), and (b) pressure plotted versus edge length (s/c)

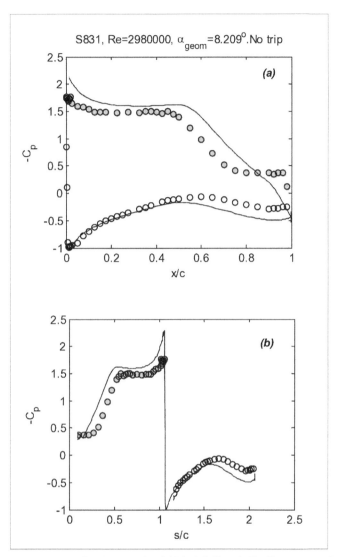

Figure 89. Mean pressure distribution on the S831 airfoil at 6.4° effective angle of attack and a Reynolds number of 2,980,000 without trip; filled symbols indicate suction side, open symbols indicate pressure side, dashed line indicates panel-method result; (a) pressure plotted versus chordwise distance (x/c), and (b) pressure plotted versus edge length (s/c)

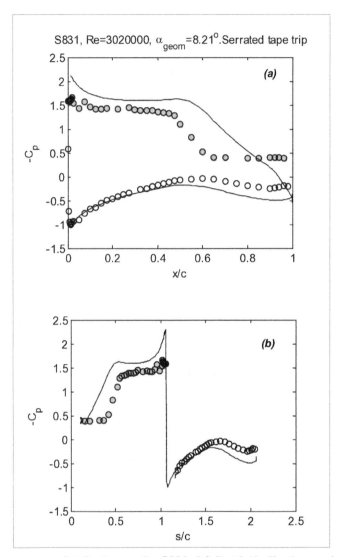

Figure 90. Mean pressure distribution on the S831 airfoil at 6.4° effective angle of attack and a Reynolds number of 3,020,000 with the serrated-tape trip; filled symbols indicate suction side, open symbols indicate pressure side, dashed line indicates panel-method result; (a) pressure plotted versus chordwise distance (x/c), and (b) pressure plotted versus edge length (s/c)

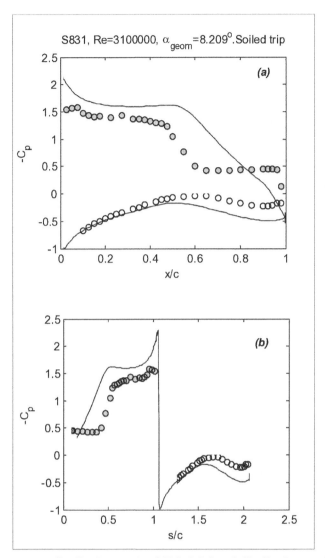

Figure 91. Mean pressure distribution on the S831 airfoil at 8.4° effective angle of attack and a Reynolds number of 3,100,000 with the soiled trip; filled symbols indicate suction side, open symbols indicate pressure side, dashed line indicates panel-method result; (a) pressure plotted versus chordwise distance (x/c), and (b) pressure plotted versus edge length (s/c)

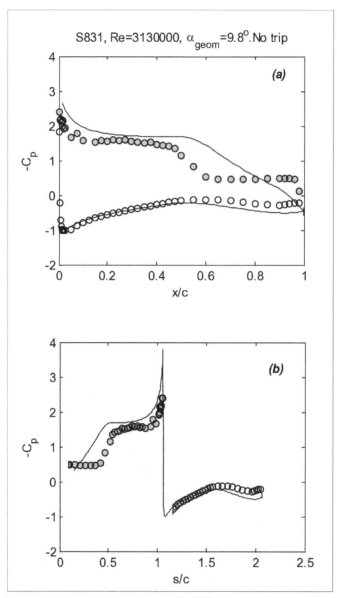

Figure 92. Mean pressure distribution on the S831 airfoil at 7.6° effective angle of attack and a Reynolds number of 3,130,000 without trip; filled symbols indicate suction side, open symbols indicate pressure side, dashed line indicates panel-method result; (a) pressure plotted versus chordwise distance (x/c), and (b) pressure plotted versus edge length (s/c)

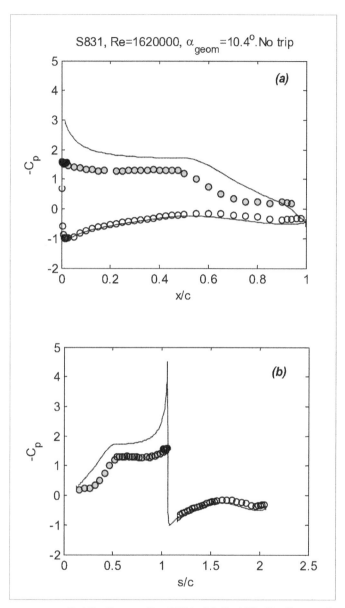

Figure 93. Mean pressure distribution on the S831 airfoil at 8° effective angle of attack and a Reynolds number of 1,620,000 without trip; filled symbols indicate suction side, open symbols indicate pressure side, dashed line indicates panel-method result; (a) pressure plotted versus chordwise distance (x/c), and (b) pressure plotted versus edge length (s/c)

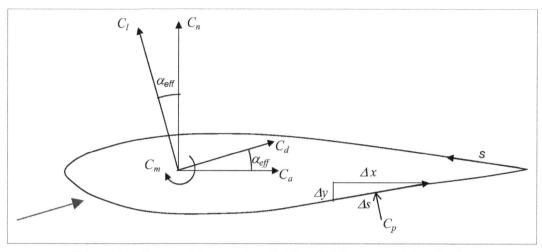

Figure 94. Definition of the edge-length (s) and of the nomenclature for the force and moment calculations

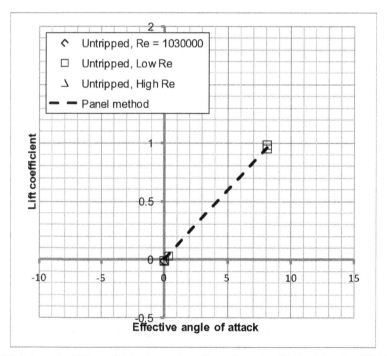

Figure 95. Integrated lift coefficient as a function of angle of attack for the NACA 0012

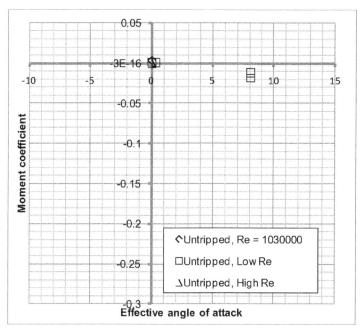

Figure 96. Integrated moment coefficient as a function of angle of attack for the NACA 0012

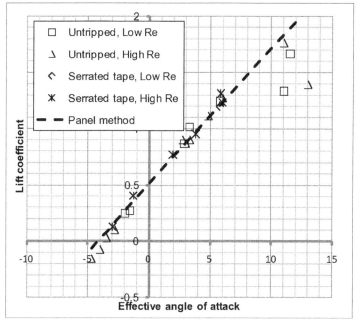

Figure 97. Integrated lift coefficient as a function of angle of attack for the B1-18

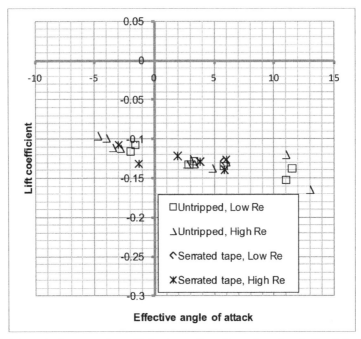

Figure 98. Integrated moment coefficient as a function of angle of attack for the B1-18

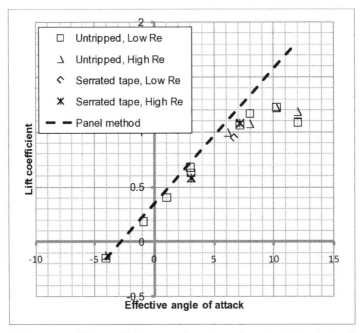

Figure 99. Integrated lift coefficient as a function of angle of attack for the DU96

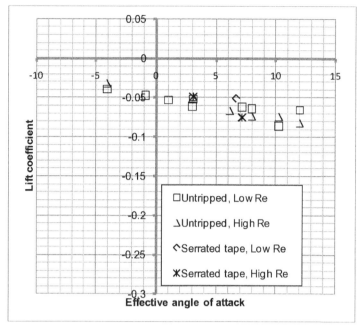

Figure 100. Integrated moment coefficient as a function of angle of attack for the DU96

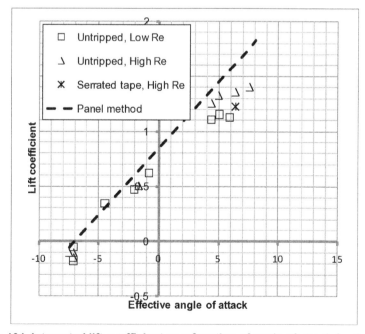

Figure 101. Integrated lift coefficient as a function of angle of attack for the S831

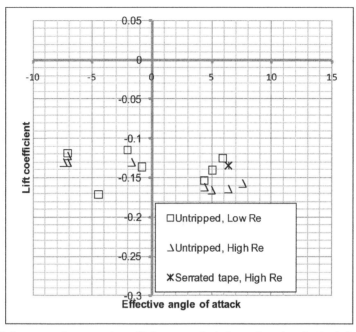

Figure 102. Integrated moment coefficient as a function of angle of attack for the S831

3.2. Wake Measurements

Stagnation pressure and static pressure profiles were measured through the airfoil wakes at $x/c = 3.74$, almost 3 chord lengths downstream of the airfoil trailing edges. Measurements were made for the B1-18, DU96, and S831 airfoils for the conditions listed in Table 7 as part of the 2 tunnel entries. For the first tunnel entry in July 2007, measurements were made with the rake mounted spanwise with the 5 probes evenly spaced near the mid-span between $Z/c = 0.042$ and 0.152. In all cases but one (discussed in detail below) the profiles measured at the 5 probe locations were identical to within the accuracy of the measurement. For the second tunnel entry in November-December 2007 the rake was mounted perpendicular to the span so that the 5 probes could be used together to measure one profile at one spanwise location ($Z/c = -0.013$) very close to mid-span. The configuration used in each case can be inferred from the dates listed in Table 7.

Table 7. Test Matrix for the Wake Measurements

Date of Measurement	Airfoil Configuration	Geometric AoA, α_g, deg.	Effective AoA, α_e, deg.	Chord Re	Trip	C_d
7/6/2007	NACA 0012	0	0	1510000	No trip	0.0059
7/6/2007	NACA 0012	10.4	8.1	1450000	No trip	0.0115
7/14/2007	B1-18	3.7	2.9	1470000	No trip	0.0089
7/14/2007	B1-18	7.4	5.8	1490000	No trip	0.0094
11/28/2007	B1-18	3.8	3	3160000	No trip	0.0062
11/28/2007	B1-18	7.7	6	3160000	No trip	0.0076
11/28/2007	B1-18	7.7	6	1650000	Serrated tape	0.0142
11/28/2007	B1-18	7.7	6	3170000	Serrated tape	0.012

Date of Measurement	Airfoil Configuration	Geometric AoA, α_g, deg.	Effective AoA, α_e, deg.	Chord Re	Trip	C_d
7/17/2007	DU96	3.9	3.1	1540000	No trip	0.0072
7/17/2007	DU96	9.2	7.2	1540000	No trip	0.0074
11/30/2007	DU96	3.9	3.05	3170000	No trip	0.0059
11/30/2007	DU96	9	7	3160000	No trip	0.006
11/30/2007	DU96	9	7	1610000	Serrated tape	0.0148
11/30/2007	DU96	9	7	3150000	Serrated tape	0.0103
11/30/2007	DU96	9	7	3120000	Soiled trip	0.0126
7/11/2007	S831	-2.6	-2	1580000	No trip	0.0078
12/3/2007	S831	-2.6	-2	3220000	No trip	0.0063
7/11/2007	S831	6.5	5.07	1570000	No trip	n/a
12/3/2007	S831	6.4	5	3220000	No trip	0.0102
12/3/2007	S831	6.4	5	3240000	Serrated tape	0.0053
12/3/2007	S831	6.4	5	3270000	Soiled trip	0.0327

Profiles of the pressure coefficients and velocity (normalized by the free-stream velocity) are plotted in Figure 103 to Figure 123 against Y position measured relative to the wake centers Y_{cl}. Pressures are plotted in terms of the following coefficients.

$$C_p = \frac{p - p_\infty}{p_{o\infty} - p_\infty}$$

$$C_{po} = \frac{p_o - p_\infty}{p_{o\infty} - p_\infty}$$

Where p_o is the measured Pitot pressure and p is the measured static pressure.

These data were used to estimate the total airfoil drag through a straightforward momentum balance. Consider the control volume shown in Figure 124.

Per unit span, the difference of the mass flowing into the volume on the left and flowing out on the right is as follows.

$$\int \rho U_\infty - \rho U \, dY$$

This, of course, is the mass flow out per unit span of the sides of the volume. The researchers assume that this occurs with an average X component of velocity of:

$$\tfrac{1}{2}(U_\infty + U_e)$$

where U_e is the potential flow velocity on the right-hand face of the volume.

Per unit span, the net *X*-momentum flux out of the volume is:

$$\rho \int U^2 - U_\infty^2 \, dY + \tfrac{1}{2}\rho(U_\infty + U_e)\int U_\infty - U \, dY$$

and the *X*-component of the pressure force on the volumes is:

$$\int p_\infty - p \, dY$$

where *p* is the pressure on the right-hand face. The total drag force per unit span on the airfoil located in the volume thus is:

$$d = \rho \int U_\infty^2 - U^2 - \tfrac{1}{2}(U_\infty + U_e)(U_\infty - U) - \frac{p - p_\infty}{\rho} \, dY$$

and the drag coefficient is as follows.

$$C_d = \int 2 - 2\frac{U^2}{U_\infty^2} - (1+\frac{U_e}{U_\infty})(1-\frac{U}{U_\infty}) - C_p \, d(Y/c)$$

In terms of the stagnation and static pressure coefficients measured on the downstream face, C_{p0} and C_p, this becomes the following.

$$C_d = \int 2 - 2(C_{p0} - C_p) - (1+\sqrt{1-C_p})(1-\sqrt{C_{p0} - C_p}) - C_p \, d(Y/c)$$
$$= \int 2 - 2C_{p0} + C_p - (1+\sqrt{1-C_p})(1-\sqrt{C_{p0} - C_p}) \, d(Y/c)$$

The integrand is zero outside the viscous wake, therefore the limits of the integral can be taken as the edges of the wake. Results of this integration are listed in Table 7 and plotted in Figure 125 to Figure 128. Note that transducer difficulties and probe-mounting issues might have influenced the static-pressure coefficients measured with the rake probes by as much as 0.05 (particularly for the first tunnel entry). As formulated above, however, the drag coefficient only is weakly dependent upon the static-pressure coefficient value. For a typical case (B1-18 airfoil at 5.8° angle of attack), changing C_p by 0.15 has less than a 3% effect on C_d.

Wake measurements on the NACA 0012 airfoil at 0° angle of attack at the lower Reynolds number of 1,510,000 (Figure 103) show a symmetric wake roughly 0.1 *c* in width and with a minimum stagnation pressure coefficient of 0.88 at its center. Not surprisingly, increasing the angle of attack to 8.1° (Figure 104) both widens and deepens the wake somewhat. These wake profiles imply drag coefficients of 0.0059 and 0.0115 respectively, values that are broadly consistent with previous 0012 measurements. Sheldahl and Klimas (1981) report values of 0.0065 and 0.0119 for a chord Reynolds number of 1,000,000.

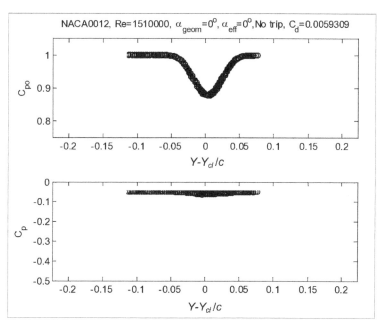

Figure 103. Stagnation and static-pressure coefficient profiles measured at X/c = 3.74 downstream of the NACA0012 at a Reynolds number of 1,510,000 and 0° effective angle of attack, no trip

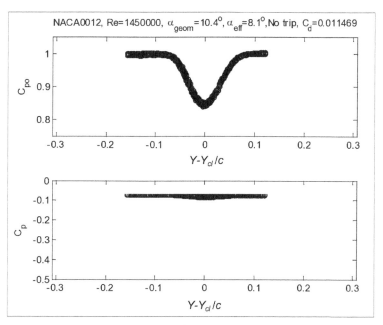

Figure 104. Stagnation and static-pressure coefficient profiles measured at X/c=3.74 downstream of the NACA 0012 at a Reynolds number of 1,450,000 and 8.1° effective angle of attack, no trip

At the lower Reynolds number, and without trip, the B1-18 airfoil (Figure 105, Figure 107) produces quite similar wakes to the NACA 0012. The drag coefficients, of 0.0089 and 0.0094 at the 2.9° and 5.8° angles of attack also are similar, bearing in mind the -4° zero-lift angle of attack for this foil.

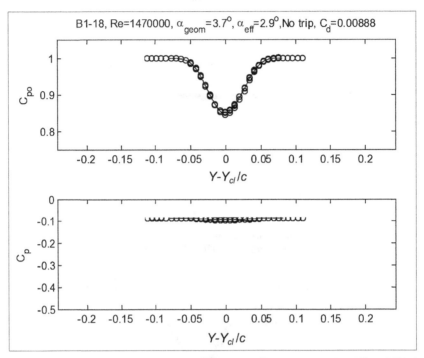

Figure 105. Stagnation and static-pressure coefficient profiles measured at *X/c* = 3.74 downstream of the B1-18 at a Reynolds number of 1,470,000 and 2.9 ° effective angle of attack, no trip

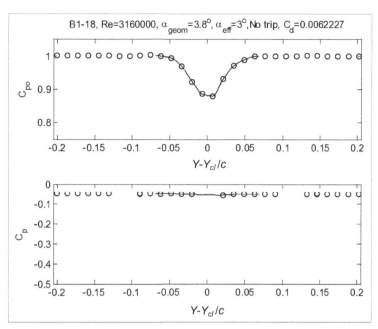

Figure 106. Stagnation and static-pressure coefficient profiles measured at X/c = 3.74 downstream of the B1-18 at a Reynolds number of 3,160,000 and 3° effective angle of attack, no trip

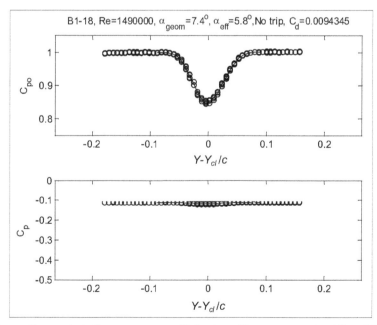

Figure 107. Stagnation and static-pressure coefficient profiles measured at X/c = 3.74 downstream of the B1-18 at a Reynolds number of 1,490,000 and 5.8° effective angle of attack, no trip

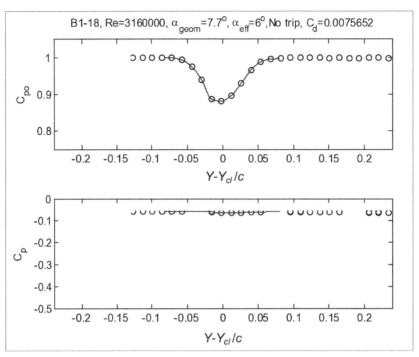

Figure 108. Stagnation and static-pressure coefficient profiles measured at X/c = 3.74 downstream of the B1-18 at a Reynolds number of 3,160,000 and 6° effective angle of attack, no trip

Doubling the Reynolds number at fixed angle of attack (compare Figure 105 and Figure 106 with Figure 107 and Figure 108) noticeably reduces the intensity and width of the wake, the corresponding drag values falling by 20% to 30% (Figure 126). Adding the serrated-tape trip widens and deepens the wake somewhat at both Reynolds numbers (Figure 109, Figure 110), increasing the drag coefficient in both cases by about 0.0045 (Figure 126). That the trip increases the drag in this way suggests that most of the drag in the untripped configuration is the result of skin friction.

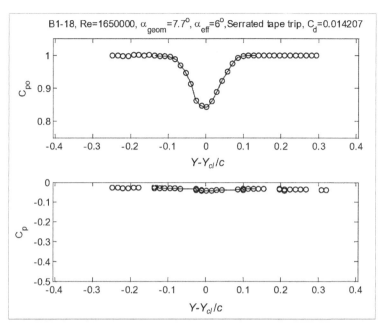

Figure 109. Stagnation and static-pressure coefficient profiles measured at X/c = 3.74 downstream of the B1-18 at a Reynolds number of 1,650,000 and 6° effective angle of attack, serrated-tape trip

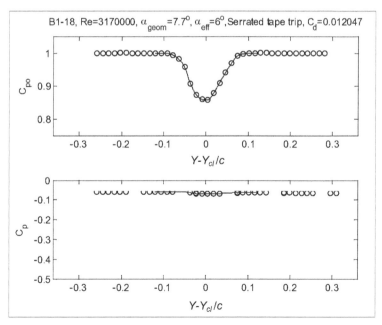

Figure 110. Stagnation and static-pressure coefficient profiles measured at X/c = 3.74 downstream of the B1-18 at a Reynolds number of 3,170,000 and 6° effective angle of attack, serrated-tape trip

Overall, the behavior of the DU96 as revealed in the wake profiles (Figure 111 to Figure 117) and in the drag coefficients (Figure 127) is quite similar to the B1-18, with the exception that the drag coefficient and wake intensity shows almost no dependence on angle of attack between 3° and 7° (zero lift angle of attack for this airfoil is -3°). As with the B1-18, adding the serrated-tape trip significantly increases the drag coefficient—by about 0.0045 at the higher Reynolds number. Interestingly, the soiled trip produces a greater drag increment (0.0066) despite its lower profile.

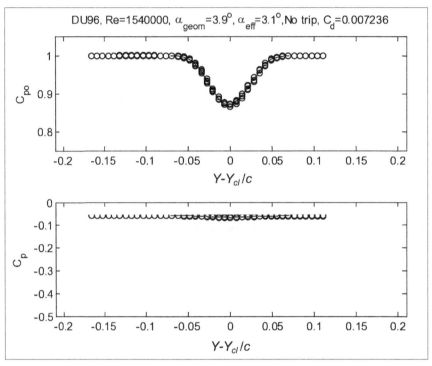

Figure 111. Stagnation and static-pressure coefficient profiles measured at X/c = 3.74 downstream of the DU96 at a Reynolds number of 1,540,000 and 3.1° effective angle of attack, no trip

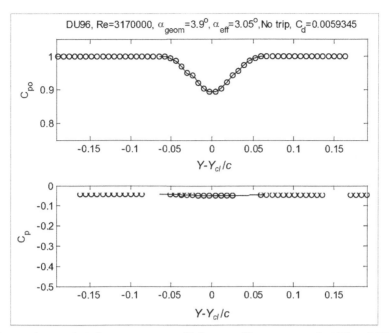

Figure 112. Stagnation and static-pressure coefficient profiles measured at _X/c_ = 3.74 downstream of the DU96 at a Reynolds number of 3,170,000 and 3° effective angle of attack, no trip

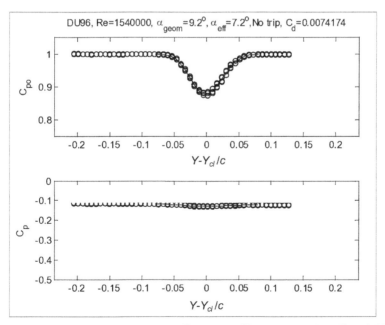

Figure 113. Stagnation and static-pressure coefficient profiles measured at X/c = 3.74 downstream of the DU96 at a Reynolds number of 1,540,000 and 7.2° effective angle of attack, no trip

120

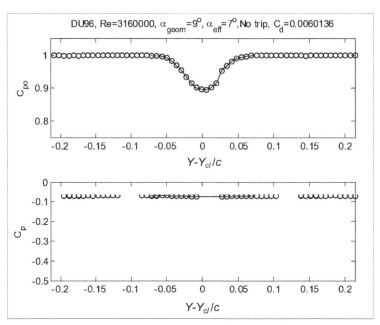

Figure 114. Stagnation and static-pressure coefficient profiles measured at *X/c* = 3.74 downstream of the DU96 at a Reynolds number of 3,160,000 and 7° effective angle of attack, no trip

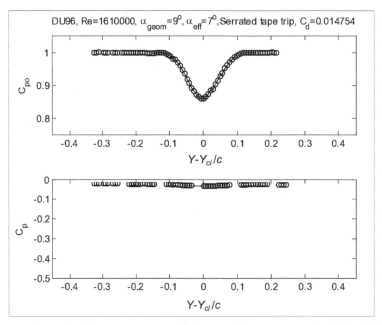

Figure 115. Stagnation and static-pressure coefficient profiles measured at *X/c* = 3.74 downstream of the DU96 at a Reynolds number of 1,610,000 and 7° effective angle of attack, serrated-tape trip

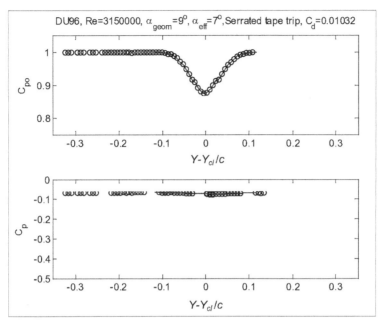

Figure 116. Stagnation and static-pressure coefficient profiles measured at X/c = 3.74 downstream of the DU96 at a Reynolds number of 3,150,000 and 7° effective angle of attack, serrated-tape trip

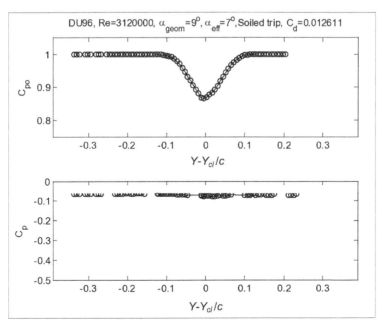

Figure 117. Stagnation and static-pressure coefficient profiles measured at X/c = 3.74 downstream of the DU96 at a Reynolds number of 3,120,000 and 7° effective angle of attack, soiled trip

At –2° angle of attack, untripped, the wake of the S831 (Figure 118, Figure 119) and the drag values it implies (Figure 128), appear unremarkable and broadly similar to those of the NACA 0012. This sense of normalcy is undermined by the remaining profile data, however. Particularly revealing are the measurements shown in Figure 120, made untripped at the lower Reynolds number and 5.1° angle of attack. These profiles were measured as part of the first tunnel entry and thus are comprised of five parallel profiles made at slightly different spanwise stations. These profiles have been distinguished in Figure 120 because they are different. At the higher spanwise stations the wake profile appears symmetric and well behaved. Moving towards mid-span, however, the profile develops a broad second minimum to the suction side of the original wake profile. This is part of the complex wake shed from the three-dimensional separation observed in the flow visualization described with the mean-pressure measurements (above). The other wake measurements made at this angle of attack (Figure 121 to Figure 123), at higher Reynolds numbers, and including the serrated and soiled trips only were measured at a single spanwise station. These profiles and the drag values they imply, however, appear erratic (drag coefficient varying by a factor of 6), presumably due to the presence of the same or a similar stall pattern. For this reason researchers think that the drag values for this airfoil—at least for 5° angle of attack—are unreliable and should be ignored because they represent only the integration of a single profile through a highly three-dimensional flow.

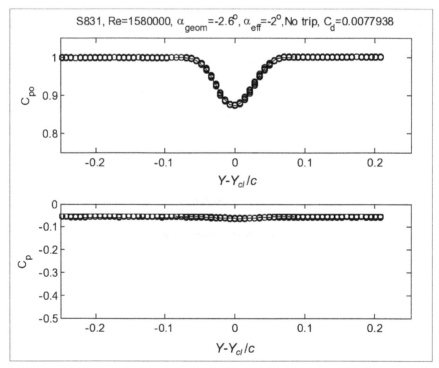

Figure 118. Stagnation and static-pressure coefficient profiles measured at *X/c* = 3.74 downstream of the S831 at a Reynolds number of 1,580,000 and –2° effective angle of attack, no trip

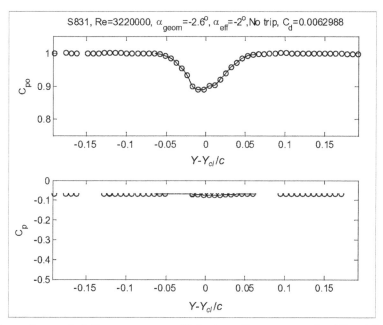

Figure 119. Stagnation and static-pressure coefficient profiles measured at X/c = 3.74 downstream of the S831 at a Reynolds number of 3,220,000 and -2° effective angle of attack, no trip

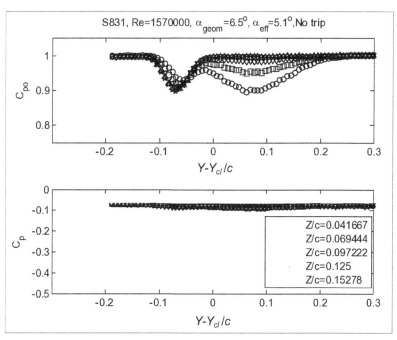

Figure 120. Stagnation and static-pressure coefficient profiles measured at X/c = 3.74 downstream of the S831 at a Reynolds number of 1,570,000 and -5° effective angle of attack, no trip

124

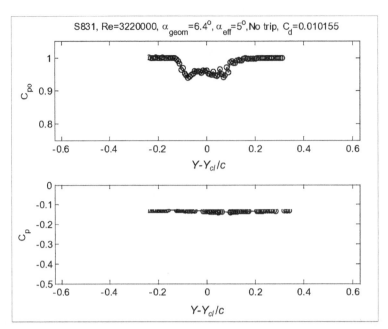

Figure 121. Stagnation and static-pressure coefficient profiles measured at X/c = 3.74 downstream of the S831 at a Reynolds number of 3,220,000 and 5° effective angle of attack, no trip

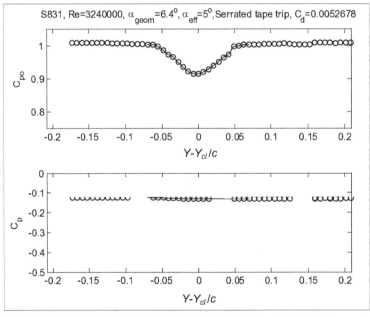

Figure 122. Stagnation and static-pressure coefficient profiles measured at X/c = 3.74 downstream of the S831 at a Reynolds number of 3,240,000 and 5° effective angle of attack, serrated-tape trip

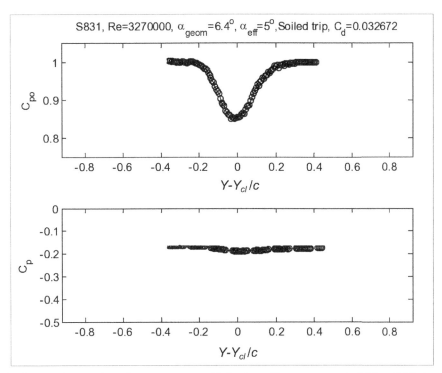

Figure 123. Stagnation and static-pressure coefficient profiles measured at X/c = 3.74 downstream of the S831 at a Reynolds number of 3,270,000 and 5° effective angle of attack, soiled trip

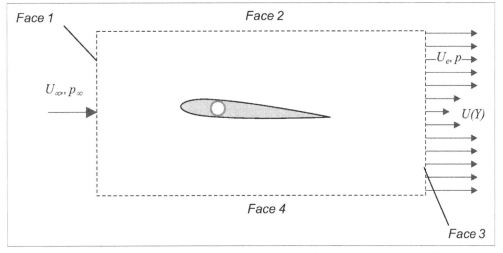

Figure 124. Control volume used for drag analysis based on wake profiles

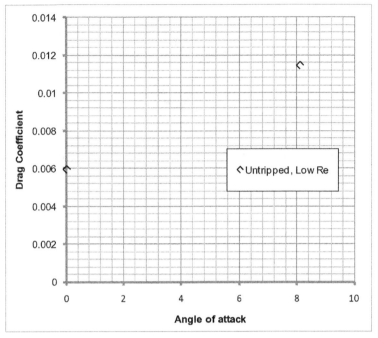

Figure 125. Integrated drag coefficient as a function of angle of attack for the NACA 0012

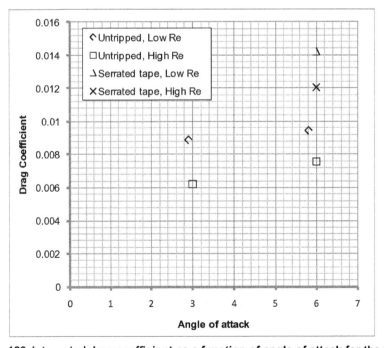

Figure 126. Integrated drag coefficient as a function of angle of attack for the B1-18

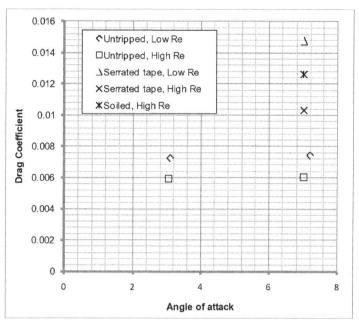

Figure 127. Integrated drag coefficient as a function of angle of attack for the DU96

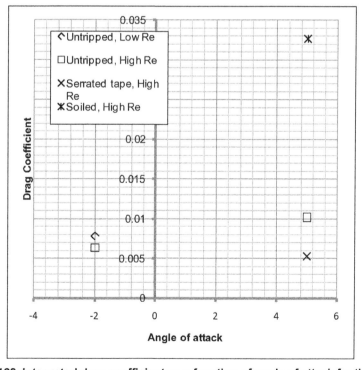

Figure 128. Integrated drag coefficient as a function of angle of attack for the S831

3.3. Trailing-Edge Boundary-Layer Properties

As discussed in Section 2 (above), a single hot-wire probe was use to measure trailing-edge boundary layers for both sides of the B1-18, DU96, and S831 airfoils. These measurements were all taken during the second wind tunnel entry in November-December 2007. Conditions and locations for the measurements, along with boundary-layer parameters, are listed in Table 8. Most measurements were made between 1.9 mm and 2.3 mm aft of the trailing edge of the airfoil to reduce the risk of probe damage. This study therefore assumes that there was no significant evolution of the boundary-layer flow over this short distance.

Table 8. Test Matrix for the Hot-Wire Measurements

	Geometric Angle of attack α_g, deg.	Effective Angle of attack α_e, deg.	Chord Re	Trip	x-x_{te} (mm)	Side	δ (mm)	δ^* (mm)	θ (mm)
B1-18	3.8	3	1,550,000	No trip	1.9	Pressure	16.9	1.6	1.2
B1-18	3.8	3	1,550,000	No trip	1.9	Suction	26.7	9.1	4.1
B1-18	3.8	3	3,160,000	No trip	1.9	Pressure	12.8	1.8	1.1
B1-18	3.8	3	3,160,000	No trip	1.9	Suction	26.1	8.8	4.0
B1-18	7.7	6	1,560,000	No trip	1.9	Pressure	14.5	1.3	0.8
B1-18	7.7	6	1,560,000	No trip	1.9	Suction	31.9	12.9	4.9
B1-18	7.7	6	1,600,000	No trip	-19	Pressure	13.9	1.3	0.9
B1-18	7.7	6	1,570,000	No trip	-19	Suction	29.0	10.6	4.6
B1-18	7.7	6	3,140,000	No trip	1.9	Pressure	11.9	1.9	1.0
B1-18	7.7	6	3,140,000	No trip	1.9	Suction	30.9	11.4	4.8
B1-18	7.7	6	3,100,000	Serrated tape	1.9	Pressure	15.5	2.5	1.4
B1-18	7.7	6	3,100,000	Serrated tape	1.9	Suction	38.7	16.1	5.8
DU96	4	3.1	1,600,000	No trip	1.9	Pressure	14.0	2.0	1.4
DU96	4	3.1	1,600,000	No trip	1.9	Suction	26.5	8.4	3.9
DU96	4	3.1	1,580,000	No trip	-16.2	Pressure	15.1	2.3	1.5
DU96	4	3.1	1,570,000	No trip	-16.2	Suction	23.6	6.2	3.5
DU96	9	7	1,560,000	No trip	1.9	Pressure	11.4	1.5	1.0
DU96	9	7	1,560,000	No trip	1.9	Suction	30.6	11.8	4.6
DU96	9	7	3,140,000	No trip	1.9	Pressure	9.7	1.9	1.0
DU96	9	7	3,140,000	No trip	1.9	Suction	23.9	8.8	3.7
DU96	9	7	3,130,000	Serrated tape	1.9	Pressure	14.0	3.3	1.6
DU96	9	7	3,130,000	Serrated tape	1.9	Suction	44.4	19.7	6.1
S831	-2.6	-2	1,550,000	No trip	2.3	Pressure	14.8	2.1	1.5
S831	-2.6	-2	1,550,000	No trip	2.3	Suction	24.7	7.9	3.6
S831	-2.6	-2	1,590,000	No trip	-16.2	Pressure	14.1	1.4	1.0
S831	-2.6	-2	1,630,000	No trip	-16.2	Suction	33.5	10.5	4.9
S831	-2.6	-2	3,130,000	No trip	2.3	Pressure	17.3	3.2	2.2
S831	-2.6	-2	3,130,000	No trip	2.3	Suction	27.1	13.4	3.6
S831	6.4	5	1,570,000	No trip	2.3	Pressure	12.6	1.0	0.5
S831	6.4	5	1,570,000	No trip	2.3	Suction	Not applicable		
S831	6.4	5	3,180,000	No trip	2.3	Pressure	8.4	1.5	0.7
S831	6.4	5	3,180,000	No trip	2.3	Suction	58.5	30.9	6.9
S831	6.4	5	1,620,000	Serrated tape	2.3	Pressure	9.0	1.1	0.6

129

	Geometric Angle of attack α_g, deg.	Effective Angle of attack α_e, deg.	Chord Re	Trip	x-x_{te} (mm)	Side	δ (mm)	δ^* (mm)	θ (mm)
S831	6.4	5	1,620,000	Serrated tape	2.3	Suction	Separated		
S831	6.4	5	3,160,000	Serrated tape	2.3	Pressure	9.8	2.3	1.1
S831	6.4	5	3,160,000	Serrated tape	2.3	Suction	Separated		

Velocity measurements are presented in Figure 129 to Figure 164. Velocities and spectral values in almost all cases are normalized on the boundary-layer edge velocity, and the y locations (measured relative to the apparent extension of the airfoil surface $|y-y_o|$) are normalized on the boundary-layer thickness values δ given in Table 8. The only exceptions are three suction-side profiles measured at 5° angle of attack at the trailing edge of the S831 airfoil (Figure 160, Figure 162, Figure 164). In these cases, the profiles indicate the presence of a region of partially or completely separated flow at the trailing edge that is too thick for the boundary-layer edge to be visible in the profile. For these cases, distances therefore are given in millimeters, and velocities and spectral values provided in terms of the velocity at the calibration point, U_{cal}.

In processing these data it was found that the boundary-layer edge location (needed to define δ and U_e) could not be inferred reliably from the mean velocity profile alone. This is because the flow velocity is not constant outside the boundary layer near the trailing edge due to the local flow curvature. This gradient tends to obscure the boundary-layer edge. Instead, the edge was defined as the location where the interpolated turbulence intensity u/U_e passes through 2%. The boundary-layer thickness was measured to this point, and the edge velocity determined from the interpolated mean velocity here. (Note that the use of the edge velocity is recursive, and so a few iterations are needed to converge to the true edge location.) For a flat plate, the location of the boundary-layer edge determined in this way, together with the location determined using the more conventional definition (point where the velocity is 99% of the uniform free stream), produce very similar answers. The displacement thickness δ^* and momentum thickness θ given in Table 8 were integrated using the usual definitions (provided below).

$$\delta^* = \int_0^\delta \left(1 - \frac{U}{U_e}\right) d|y - y_0|$$

$$\theta = \int_0^\delta \frac{U}{U_e}\left(1 - \frac{U}{U_e}\right) d|y - y_0|$$

Measurements were made just downstream of the trailing edge, therefore points were measured close to or below the level of the airfoil trailing-edge surface, where the flow clearly was not representative of the boundary layer upstream. Measurements at these points are shown in the plots using grey symbols, and were not included in the integral thickness calculations. In all cases where measurements were made downstream of the trailing edge, the profiles themselves (e.g., Figure 129, Figure 130) provide a fairly clear indication of the position y_o of the origin of the boundary-layer profile on both sides of the trailing edge. In most cases (but not in all) this position agreed within a fraction of a millimeter with the origin of the hot-wire traverse, which was set (by eye) with the hot-wire in line with the center of the trailing edge. (Note that some adjustment would be expected even if the alignment were perfect, given the finite thickness of

130

the trailing edges and uncertainty in the flow direction immediately downstream). For the profiles measured upstream of the trailing edge, the origin of the traverse was set using the point where the hot-wire probe stem made contact with the airfoil surface and the probe geometry. In two cases (shown in Figure 134 and Figure 154) this position was inferred after the fact from the apparent reversal of the near-wall velocity gradient generated by the deflection of the probe stem after contacting the surface.

At 3° angle of attack and a Reynolds number of 1,500,000 without trip the structure of the trailing-edge boundary layers on the B1-18 airfoil (Figure 129, Figure 130) betrays the pressure gradient history that they have experienced over the upstream surfaces of the airfoil, visible in Figure 42. The pressure-side mean-velocity profile (Figure 129) appears quite full (resulting in quite low displacement and momentum thicknesses as compared to δ, see Table 8) presumably because of the strong favorable pressure gradient it experiences over the last 20% chord of the airfoil. The distribution of turbulence intensity in the layer, however, is not typical of a purely accelerated boundary layer. The profile shows a bulge of higher turbulence levels near the mid-height of the boundary layer, which could well be a remnant of flow structure produced by the adverse pressure gradient imposed between the 30% and 80% chord locations. Velocity spectra measured throughout the boundary layer have a fairly typical turbulent character and display an inertial subrange (of -5/3 slope) and a high-frequency roll off. There is no evidence of periodic behavior such as vortex shedding.

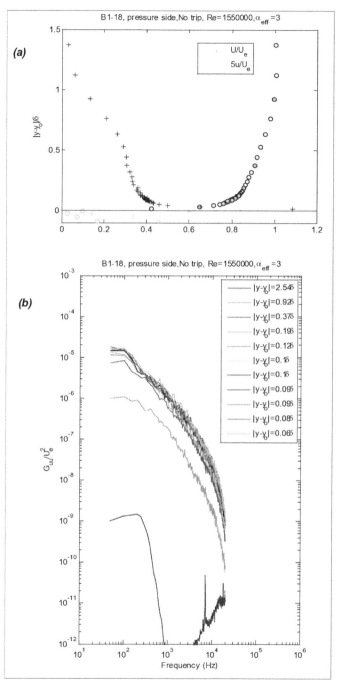

Figure 129. Velocity measurements on the pressure side of the B1-18 airfoil 1.9 mm downstream of the trailing edge at a Reynolds number of 1,550,000 and 3° effective angle of attack, no trip; (a) normalized profiles of mean velocity and turbulence intensity, (b) autospectra of velocity fluctuations at selected profile locations

The suction-side boundary layer (Figure 130) is about 60% thicker than the pressure side but its displacement and momentum thicknesses are three to five times as large, reflecting the much lower momentum in the mean-velocity profile. The long and nearly constant adverse pressure gradient experienced by this layer over the last 80% of the foil is responsible for this loss of momentum and the higher turbulence levels that are felt throughout this layer. There is no evidence of separation in either the mean-velocity or turbulence-intensity profiles. Spectra in the boundary layer show a longer inertial subrange than that of the pressure side.

Increasing the angle of attack increases the intensity of the pressure gradients on both sides of the foil, but does not change their qualitative character (Figure 42 to Figure 47). Not surprisingly, therefore, the pressure-side boundary layer (Figure 131) becomes more full and its displacement and momentum thicknesses fall (Table 8), whereas the reverse effects are seen in the suction-side boundary layer (Figure 132). The spectral character of the boundary-layer velocity fluctuations does not appear to change much, with the exception of the appearance of additional energy at low-frequencies (< 200 Hz) in the spectrum measured closest to the bottom of the boundary layer on the pressure side (Figure 131). These elevated levels likely are not a feature of the flow but the result of slight vibration of the probe stem combined with the steep near-wall velocity gradients that characterize this accelerated flow. These measurements, for 6° angle of attack, were measured both downstream (Figure 131, Figure 132) and upstream (Figure 133, Figure 134) of the trailing edge. The profiles and boundary-layer parameters (Table 8) show remarkably little evolution of the boundary layers as they cross the trailing edge. The largest difference (in the peak level of the turbulence intensity on the suction side) might have more to do with the evolution or selection of the normalizing edge velocity than any absolute change in the boundary-layer structure. The close agreement between the integral boundary-layer parameters (Table 8) obtained upstream and downstream of the trailing edge is probably spurious. Both the momentum and displacement thickness values depend heavily on the nearest wall part of the profile which is inevitably missing for the profiles measured upstream of the trailing edge. The integral thickness values for these cases thus have significant additional uncertainty associated with the interpolation assumed in this region.

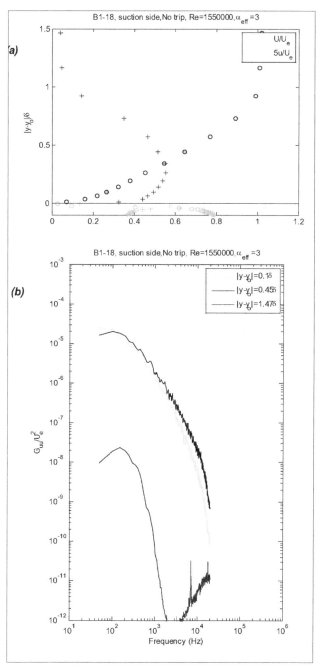

Figure 130. Velocity measurements on the suction side of the B1-18 airfoil 1.9 mm downstream of the trailing edge at a Reynolds number of 1,550,000 and 3° effective angle of attack, no trip; (a) normalized profiles of mean velocity and turbulence intensity; (b) autospectra of velocity fluctuations at selected profile locations

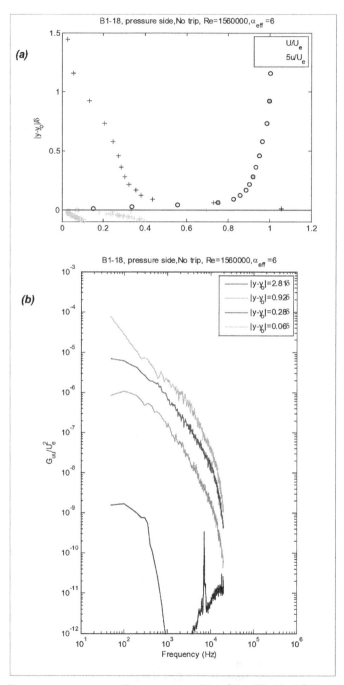

Figure 131. Velocity measurements on the pressure side of the B1-18 airfoil 1.9 mm downstream of the trailing edge at a Reynolds number of 1,560,000 and 6° effective angle of attack, no trip; (a) normalized profiles of mean velocity and turbulence intensity; (b) autospectra of velocity fluctuations at selected profile locations

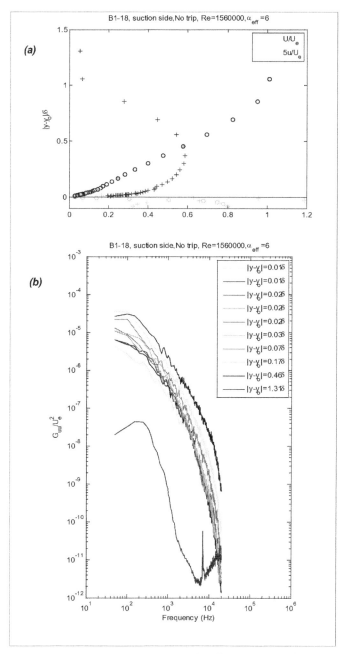

Figure 132. Velocity measurements on the suction side of the B1-18 airfoil 1.9 mm downstream of the trailing edge at a Reynolds number of 1,560,000 and 6° effective angle of attack, no trip; (a) normalized profiles of mean velocity and turbulence intensity; (b) autospectra of velocity fluctuations at selected profile locations

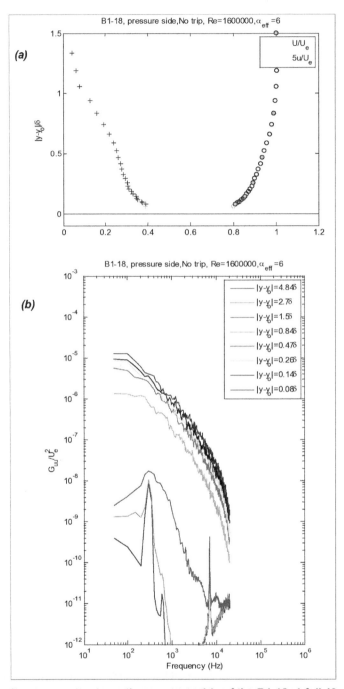

Figure 133. Velocity measurements on the pressure side of the B1-18 airfoil 19 mm upstream of the trailing edge at a Reynolds number of 1,600,000 and 6° effective angle of attack, no trip; (a) normalized profiles of mean velocity and turbulence intensity; (b) autospectra of velocity fluctuations at selected profile locations

137

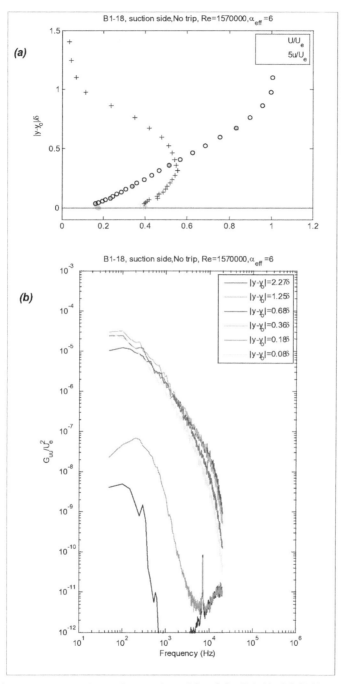

Figure 134. Velocity measurements on the suction side of the B1-18 airfoil 19 mm upstream of the trailing edge at a Reynolds number of 1,570,000 and 6° effective angle of attack, no trip; (a) normalized profiles of mean velocity and turbulence intensity; (b) autospectra of velocity fluctuations at selected profile locations

Figure 135 to Figure 138 show the same sequence of boundary-layer profiles but at double the Reynolds number. The suction-side profiles (Figure 136, Figure 138) and the associated boundary-layer parameters (Table 8) show almost no effect of Reynolds number. Effects on the pressure-side profiles are dominated by the near-wall region where the increase in Reynolds number, rather surprisingly, produces a decrease in the near-wall velocity gradient. The velocity spectra on both sides of the foil show the inertial subrange extending to higher frequencies (indicating a higher-turbulence Reynolds number). Those on the pressure side reveal increased effects of probe vibration in this higher-speed flow. Effects of adding the serrated-tape trip at the higher Reynolds number are barely discernable in the normalized profiles (compare Figure 137 and Figure 138 with Figure 139 and Figure 140). The boundary-layer parameters (*see* Table 8) reveal, however, that both boundary layers are about 25% thicker with the trip.

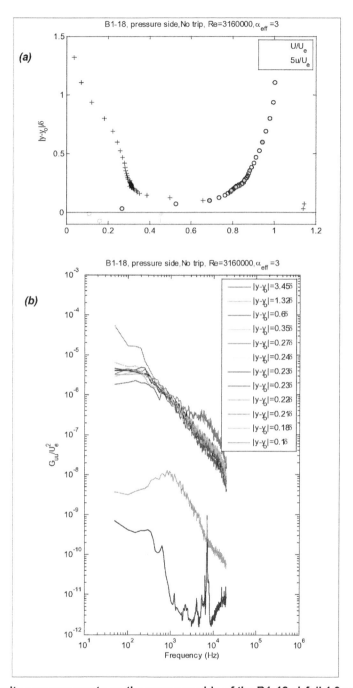

Figure 135. Velocity measurements on the pressure side of the B1-18 airfoil 1.9 mm downstream of the trailing edge at a Reynolds number of 3,160,000 and 3° effective angle of attack, no trip; (a) normalized profiles of mean velocity and turbulence intensity;(b) autospectra of velocity fluctuations at selected profile locations

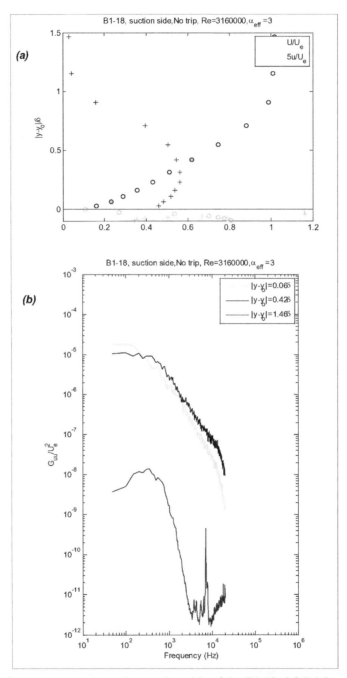

Figure 136. Velocity measurements on the suction side of the B1-18 airfoil 1.9 mm downstream of the trailing edge at a Reynolds number of 3,160,000 and 3° effective angle of attack, no trip; (a) normalized profiles of mean velocity and turbulence intensity; (b) autospectra of velocity fluctuations at selected profile locations

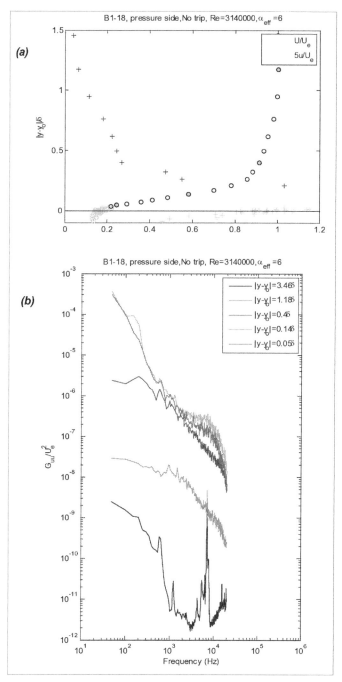

Figure 137. Velocity measurements on the pressure side of the B1-18 airfoil 1.9 mm downstream of the trailing edge at a Reynolds number of 3,140,000 and 6° effective angle of attack, no trip; (a) normalized profiles of mean velocity and turbulence intensity; (b) autospectra of velocity fluctuations at selected profile locations

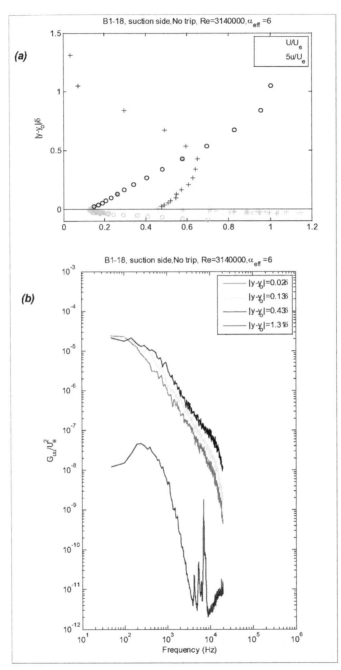

Figure 138. Velocity measurements on the suction side of the B1-18 airfoil 1.9 mm downstream of the trailing edge at a Reynolds number of 3,140,000 and 6° effective angle of attack, no trip; (a) normalized profiles of mean velocity and turbulence intensity; (b) autospectra of velocity fluctuations at selected profile locations

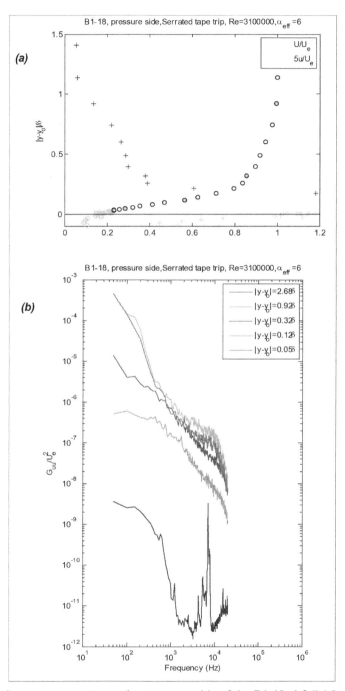

Figure 139. Velocity measurements on the pressure side of the B1-18 airfoil 1.9 mm downstream of the trailing edge at a Reynolds number of 3,100,000 and 6° effective angle of attack, serrated-tape trip; (a) normalized profiles of mean velocity and turbulence intensity; (b) autospectra of velocity fluctuations at selected profile locations

144

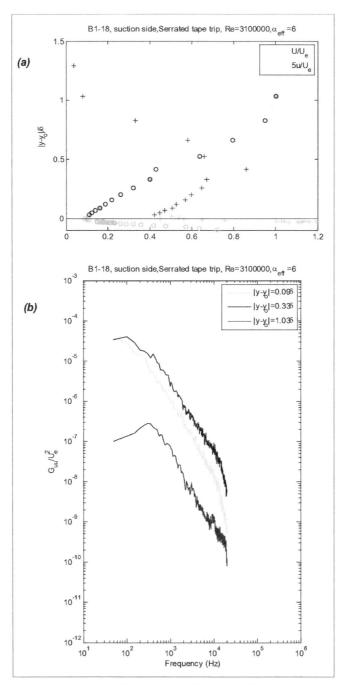

Figure 140. Velocity measurements on the suction side of the B1-18 airfoil 1.9 mm downstream of the trailing edge at a Reynolds number of 3,100,000 and 6° effective angle of attack, serrated-tape trip; (a) normalized profiles of mean velocity and turbulence intensity; (b) autospectra of velocity fluctuations at selected profile locations

The measurements made upstream and downstream of the trailing edge of the DU96 airfoil (Figure 141 through Figure 144) show that here too, there is very little change in the quantitative or qualitative flow structure in the immediate vicinity of the trailing edge. As with the B1-18, there is a small change (increase) in the peak turbulence levels on the suction side as the trailing edge is passed which we attribute to a change in the U_e scale. Again, note that the integral thicknesses (Table 8) probably are more reliable for the profiles measured downstream.

The qualitative form of the boundary-layer profiles for the DU96 and their behavior with angle of attack and Reynolds number is quite similar to that seen for the B1-18. At 3.1° (Figure 141, Figure 142) the pressure-side boundary layer clearly is much fuller and thinner than the suction-side layer, and the overall boundary-layer thicknesses are similar to those seen on the B1-18 at this condition (Table 8). Increasing the angle of attack to 7° (Figure 145, Figure 146) further emphasizes the differences between the two sides. Increasing the Reynolds number (Figure 147, Figure 148), as with the B1-18, again has its largest effect on reducing the near-wall velocity gradient in the pressure-side boundary layer. The serrated-tape trip (Figure 149, Figure 150) again produces a significant thickening of the boundary layer on both sides of the airfoil. For the DU96, however, the trip changes the character of the suction-side mean velocity profile, introducing a distinct inflection that suggests that the flow is at or near separation.

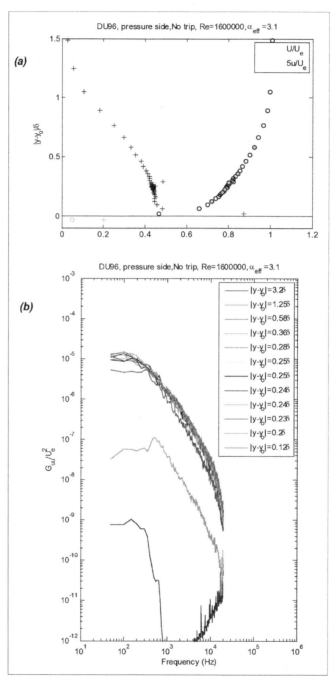

Figure 141. Velocity measurements on the pressure side of the DU96 airfoil 1.9 mm downstream of the trailing edge at a Reynolds number of 1,600,000 and 3.1° effective angle of attack, serrated-tape trip; (a) normalized profiles of mean velocity and turbulence intensity; (b) autospectra of velocity fluctuations at selected profile locations

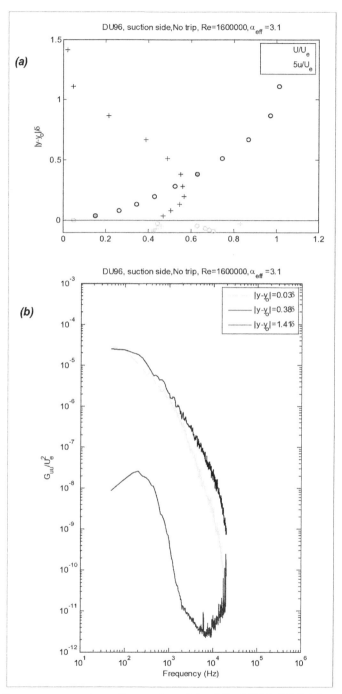

Figure 142. Velocity measurements on the suction side of the DU96 airfoil 1.9 mm downstream of the trailing edge at a Reynolds number of 1,600,000 and 3.1° effective angle of attack, serrated-tape trip; (a) normalized profiles of mean velocity and turbulence intensity; (b) autospectra of velocity fluctuations at selected profile locations

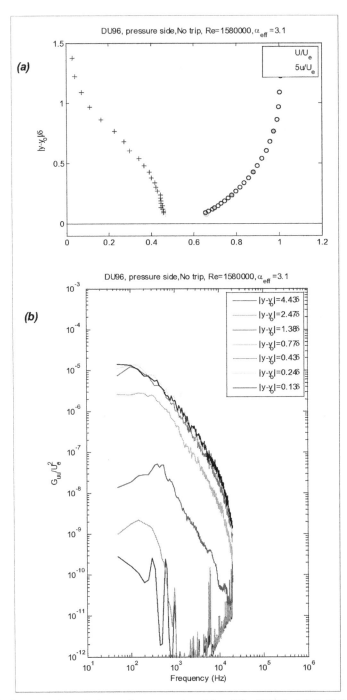

Figure 143. Velocity measurements on the pressure side of the DU96 airfoil 16.2 mm upstream of the trailing edge at a Reynolds number of 1,580,000 and 3.1° effective angle of attack, no trip; (a) normalized profiles of mean velocity and turbulence intensity; (b) autospectra of velocity fluctuations at selected profile locations

149

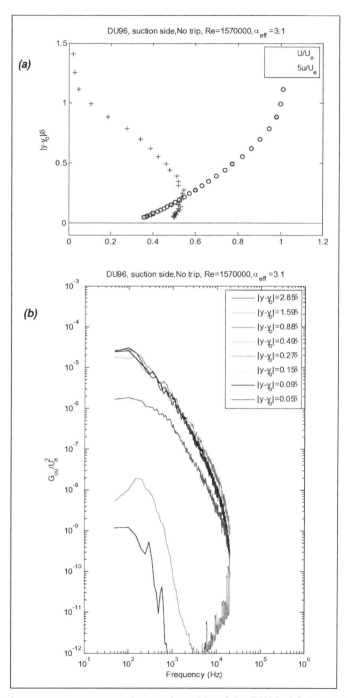

Figure 144. Velocity measurements on the suction side of the DU96 airfoil 16.2 mm upstream of the trailing edge at a Reynolds number of 1,570,000 and 3.1° effective angle of attack, no trip; (a) normalized profiles of mean velocity and turbulence intensity; (b) autospectra of velocity fluctuations at selected profile locations

150

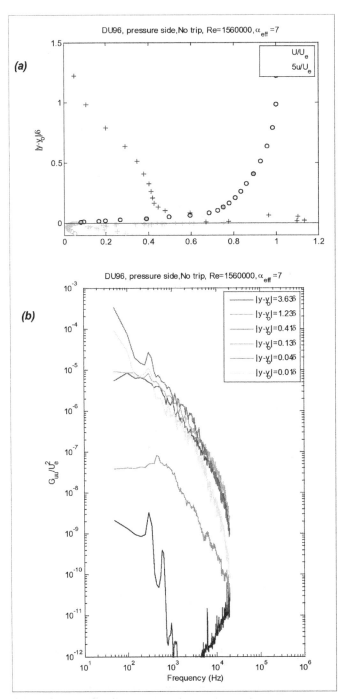

Figure 145. Velocity measurements on the pressure side of the DU96 airfoil 1.9 mm downstream of the trailing edge at a Reynolds number of 1,560,000 and 7° effective angle of attack, no trip; (a) normalized profiles of mean velocity and turbulence intensity; (b) autospectra of velocity fluctuations at selected profile locations

151

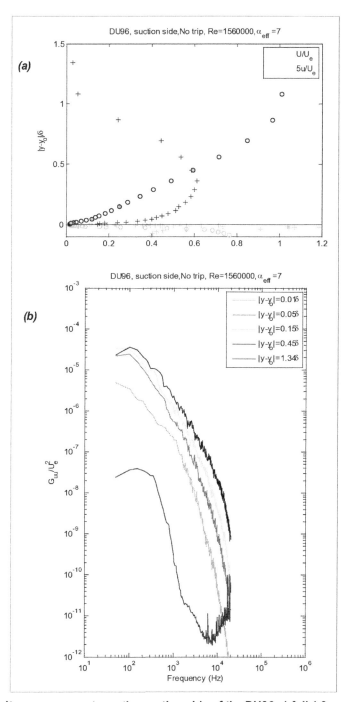

Figure 146. Velocity measurements on the suction side of the DU96 airfoil 1.9 mm downstream of the trailing edge at a Reynolds number of 1,560,000 and 7° effective angle of attack, no trip; (a) normalized profiles of mean velocity and turbulence intensity; (b) autospectra of velocity fluctuations at selected profile locations

152

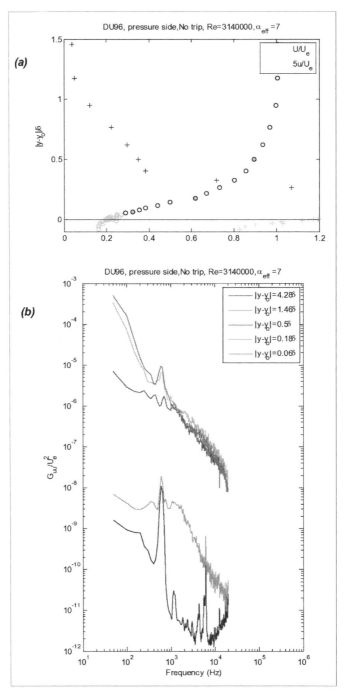

Figure 147. Velocity measurements on the pressure side of the DU96 airfoil 1.9 mm downstream of the trailing edge at a Reynolds number of 3,140,000 and 7° effective angle of attack, no trip; (a) normalized profiles of mean velocity and turbulence intensity; (b) autospectra of velocity fluctuations at selected profile locations

153

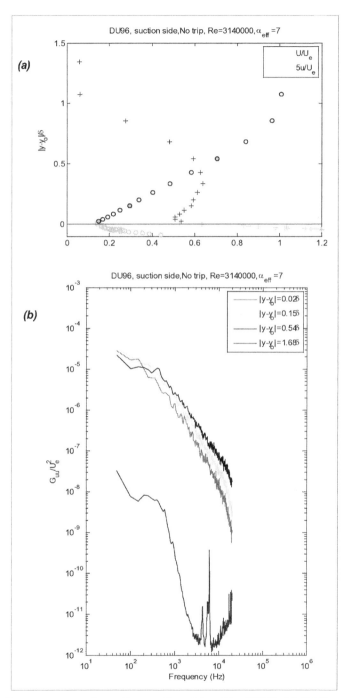

Figure 148. Velocity measurements on the suction side of the DU96 airfoil 1.9 mm downstream of the trailing edge at a Reynolds number of 3,140,000 and 7° effective angle of attack, no trip; (a) normalized profiles of mean velocity and turbulence intensity; (b) autospectra of velocity fluctuations at selected profile locations

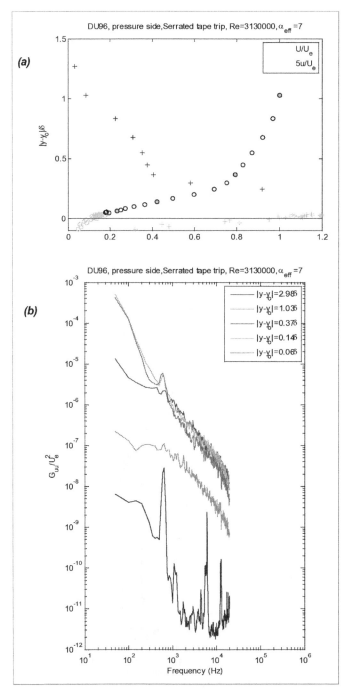

Figure 149. Velocity measurements on the pressure side of the DU96 airfoil 1.9 mm downstream of the trailing edge at a Reynolds number of 3,130,000 and 7° effective angle of attack, serrated-tape trip; (a) normalized profiles of mean velocity and turbulence intensity; (b) autospectra of velocity fluctuations at selected profile locations

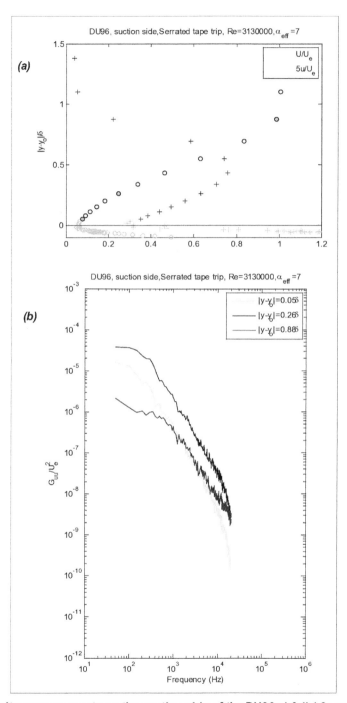

Figure 150. Velocity measurements on the suction side of the DU96 airfoil 1.9 mm downstream of the trailing edge at a Reynolds number of 3,130,000 and 7° effective angle of attack, serrated-tape trip; (a) normalized profiles of mean velocity and turbulence intensity; (b) autospectra of velocity fluctuations at selected profile locations

The S831 boundary-layer profiles measured at -2° angle of attack at the lower Reynolds number (Figure 151 to Figure 154) show the bigger change in the flow as it passes the trailing edge, than with the other two airfoils. The pressure-side boundary layer, in particular, appears slightly fuller measured downstream of the trailing edge than upstream. The unconventional behavior of the S831 airfoil is as apparent in the boundary-layer measurements as in the wakes and pressure distributions described above. Doubling the Reynolds number at -2° (compare Figure 151 and Figure 152 with Figure 157 and Figure 158) significantly increases the boundary-layer thickness and reduces the fullness of the mean velocity profiles on both sides. Indeed, on the suction side the change is from a clearly attached adverse-pressure gradient type profile (Figure 152), to one that strongly suggests separation (Figure 158). At 5° angle of attack, regardless of trip (Figure 159 to Figure 164) the suction-side profiles either show the flow to be partially or completely stalled, consistent with the wake measurements discussed above. The velocity spectra measured in the pressure-side boundary-layer profiles at 5° are by far the most affected by probe vibration, therefore observations concerning the detailed near-wall properties of these boundary layers probably should be made with caution. It is clear from the overall form of these profiles, however, that in all of these cases the pressure-side boundary layer is attached and quite thin.

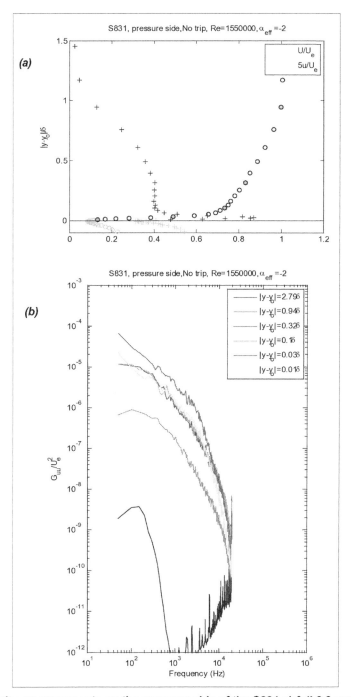

Figure 151. Velocity measurements on the pressure side of the S831 airfoil 2.3 mm downstream of the trailing edge at a Reynolds number of 1,550,000 and -2° effective angle of attack, no trip; (a) normalized profiles of mean velocity and turbulence intensity; (b) autospectra of velocity fluctuations at selected profile locations

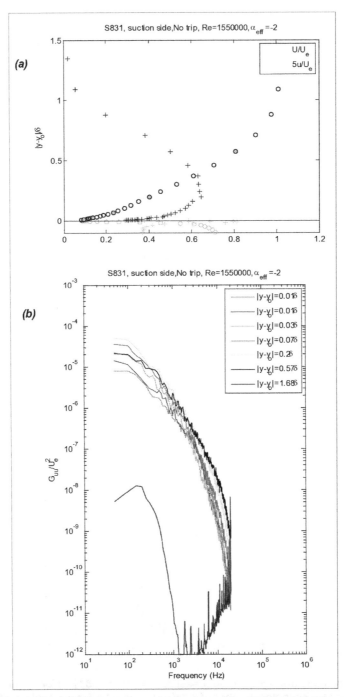

Figure 152. Velocity measurements on the suction side of the S831 airfoil 2.3 mm downstream of the trailing edge at a Reynolds number of 1,550,000 and -2° effective angle of attack, no trip; (a) normalized profiles of mean velocity and turbulence intensity; (b) autospectra of velocity fluctuations at selected profile locations

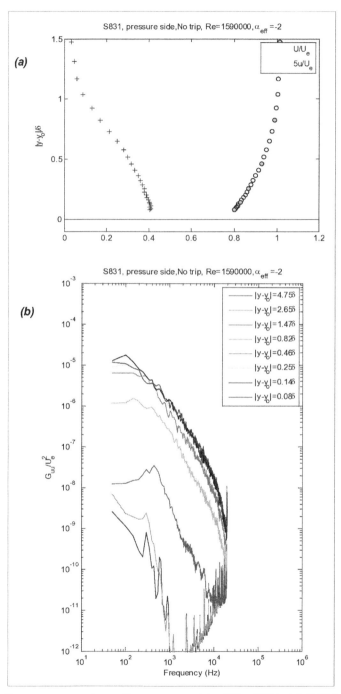

Figure 153. Velocity measurements on the pressure side of the S831 airfoil 16.2 mm upstream of the trailing edge at a Reynolds number of 1,590,000 and -2° effective angle of attack, no trip; (a) normalized profiles of mean velocity and turbulence intensity; (b) autospectra of velocity fluctuations at selected profile locations

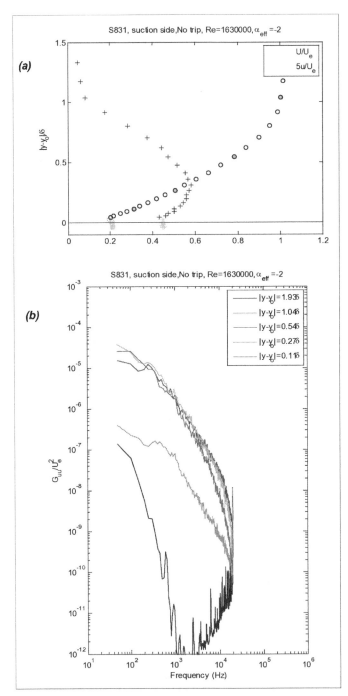

Figure 154. Velocity measurements on the suction side of the S831 airfoil 16.2 mm upstream of the trailing edge at a Reynolds number of 1,630,000 and -2° effective angle of attack, no trip; (a) normalized profiles of mean velocity and turbulence intensity; (b) autospectra of velocity fluctuations at selected profile locations

161

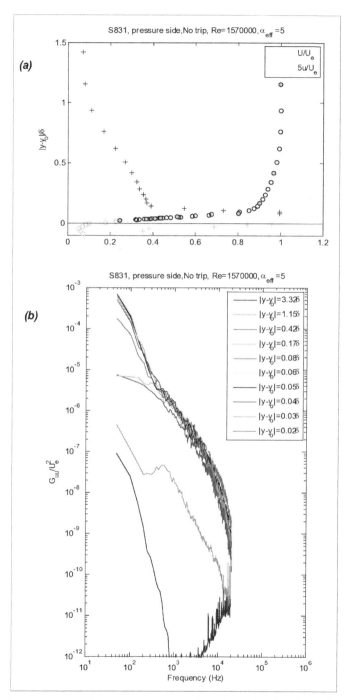

Figure 155. Velocity measurements on the pressure side of the S831 airfoil 2.3 mm downstream of the trailing edge at a Reynolds number of 1,570,000 and 5° effective angle of attack, no trip; (a) normalized profiles of mean velocity and turbulence intensity; (b) autospectra of velocity fluctuations at selected profile locations

162

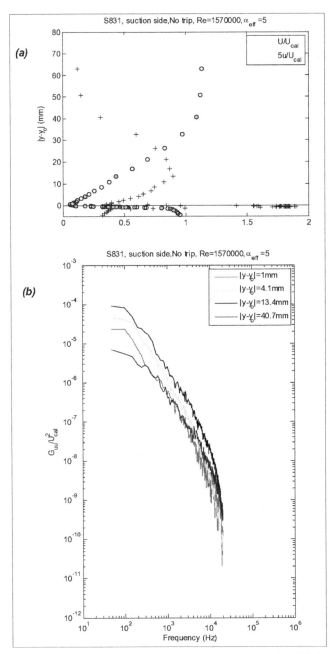

Figure 156. Velocity measurements on the suction side of the S831 airfoil 2.3 mm downstream of
the trailing edge at a Reynolds number of 1,570,000 and 5° effective angle of attack, no trip;
(a) normalized profiles of mean velocity and turbulence intensity; (b) autospectra of velocity
fluctuations at selected profile locations (note thick flow preventing determination of, and
normalization on, boundary-layer parameters)

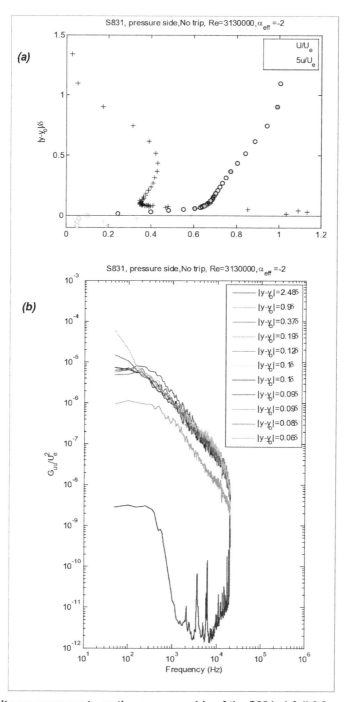

Figure 157. Velocity measurements on the pressure side of the S831 airfoil 2.3 mm downstream of the trailing edge at a Reynolds number of 3,130,000 and -2° effective angle of attack, no trip; (a) normalized profiles of mean velocity and turbulence intensity; (b) autospectra of velocity fluctuations at selected profile locations

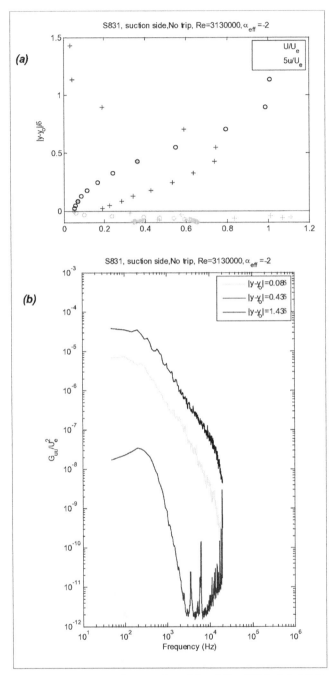

Figure 158. Velocity measurements on the suction side of the S831 airfoil 2.3 mm downstream of the trailing edge at a Reynolds number of 3,130,000 and -2° effective angle of attack, no trip; (a) normalized profiles of mean velocity and turbulence intensity; (b) autospectra of velocity fluctuations at selected profile locations

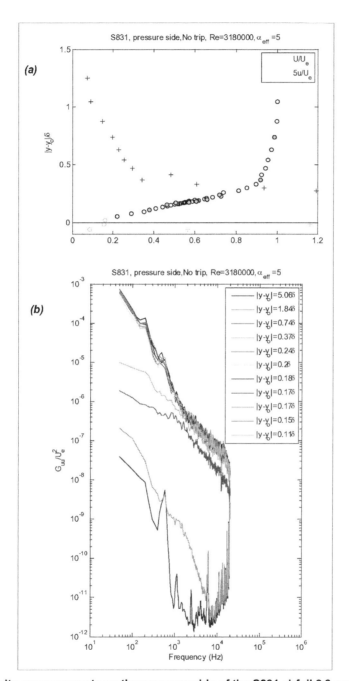

Figure 159. Velocity measurements on the pressure side of the S831 airfoil 2.3 mm downstream of the trailing edge at a Reynolds number of 3,180,000 and 5° effective angle of attack, no trip; (a) normalized profiles of mean velocity and turbulence intensity; (b) autospectra of velocity fluctuations at selected profile locations

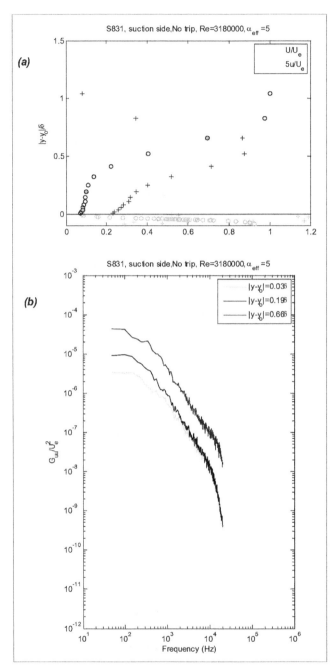

Figure 160. Velocity measurements on the suction side of the S831 airfoil 2.3 mm downstream of the trailing edge at a Reynolds number of 3,180,000 and 5° effective angle of attack, no trip; (a) normalized profiles of mean velocity and turbulence intensity; (b) autospectra of velocity fluctuations at selected profile locations

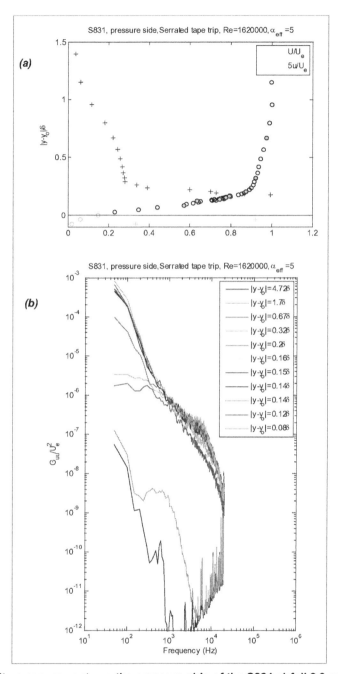

Figure 161. Velocity measurements on the pressure side of the S831 airfoil 2.3 mm downstream of the trailing edge at a Reynolds number of 1,620,000 and 5° effective angle of attack, serrated-tape trip; (a) normalized profiles of mean velocity and turbulence intensity; (b) autospectra of velocity fluctuations at selected profile locations

168

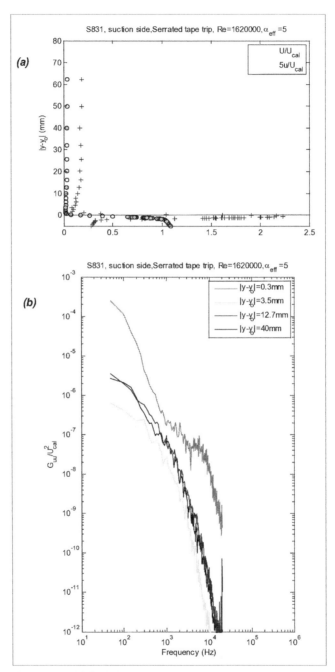

Figure 162. Velocity measurements on the suction side of the S831 airfoil 2.3 mm downstream of the trailing edge at a Reynolds number of 1,620,000 and 5° effective angle of attack, serrated-tape trip; (a) normalized profiles of mean velocity and turbulence intensity; (b) autospectra of velocity fluctuations at selected profile locations (note thick separated flow preventing determination of, and normalization on, boundary-layer parameters)

169

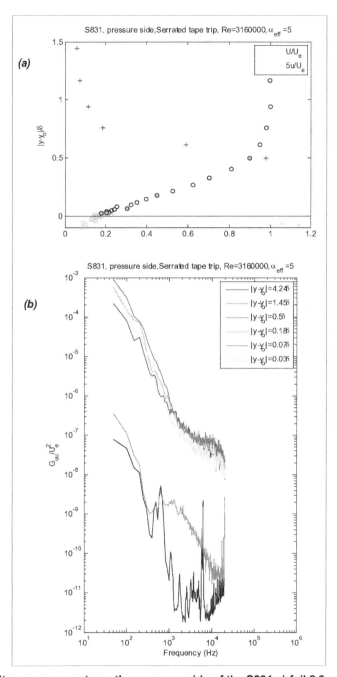

Figure 163. Velocity measurements on the pressure side of the S831 airfoil 2.3 mm downstream of the trailing edge at a Reynolds number of 3,160,000 and 5° effective angle of attack, serrated tape trip; (a) normalized profiles of mean velocity and turbulence intensity; (b) autospectra of velocity fluctuations at selected profile locations

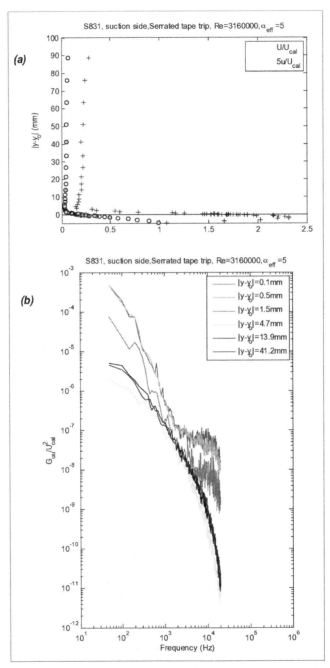

Figure 164. Velocity measurements on the suction side of the S831 airfoil 2.3 mm downstream of the trailing edge at a Reynolds number of 3,160,000 and 5° effective angle of attack, serrated-tape trip; (a) normalized profiles of mean velocity and turbulence intensity; (b) autospectra of velocity fluctuations at selected profile locations (note thick separated flow preventing determination of, and normalization on, boundary-layer parameters)

4. Acoustic Results and Discussions

The data from the 63 microphones in the arrays were processed to compute the following results.

4.1. Average Noise Spectrum

The average spectrum of all 63 microphones in the array was computed. It provides an estimate of the noise inside the anechoic chamber. It is useful to obtain noise results at low frequency, below 500 Hz, where the array resolution is very poor and noise maps are not computed. Strong vortex shedding occurring below 500 Hz has been successfully measured from some airfoils with blunt trailing edge (Devenport and Burdisso 2008). For the airfoils tested here, data from the average spectrum prove useful only for the large chord NACA 0012 airfoil at an angle of attack greater than 4° and 28 m/s flow speed. For these few cases, vortex shedding takes place and the fundamental shedding frequency occurs below 500 Hz. The average spectrum was computed in narrow band (3.125 Hz resolution) and in one-twelfth octave bands. The one-twelfth octave band data were obtained by adding spectral lines within the band. The definition of the one-twelfth octave bands used here is described in Appendix B.

4.2. Acoustic Maps

The acoustic maps were computed over a plane along the center of the test section as illustrated in Figure 165(a). The acoustic maps were computed for the one-twelfth octave bands in the 500 Hz to 5,000 Hz range. The beamforming grid has 201 points along the test-section direction (grid resolution of 2.54 cm) and 73 points from floor to ceiling (grid resolution of 2.54 cm) for a total of 14,600 grid points. The color contours in the acoustic maps range from the maximum level in the map down to 10 dB as illustrated in Figure 165(b). The level (color) in the acoustic maps represents the noise observed at the array plane due to sources at the grid points.

4.3. Integrated Spectrum

Using the point-spread function, the levels in the scanning grid encompassing the trailing edge were summed to a single value for each frequency to compute the integrated spectrum. In this work, the levels were integrated 5 dB down from the peak value to avoid adding the effects of the sidelobes from other sources. The integrated spectrum was computed for all the con-figurations in one-twelfth octave bands in the 500 Hz to 5,000 Hz range. To compute the integrated spectrum, a volume enclosing the trailing edge of the airfoil was defined for the beamforming-integration process. The volume for the integration is shown in Figure 166. The volume has a square cross section and it is aligned with the airfoil trailing edge (Figure 166, green box). The parts of the trailing edge next to the junction with the tunnel were excluded to avoid noise due to end effects as well as other spurious noise sources seen on the test-section floor and ceiling. Therefore, the integrated spectrum represents the trailing-edge noise radiated by the center two-thirds of the airfoil as measured at the array position. The noise levels are presented as un-weighted decibels reference to 20×10^{-6} Pa.

For the sake of completeness and to provide additional insight, the integrated spectra were normalized and presented in Appendix C. The noise levels were scaled using the free-stream velocity using the fifth power law. Prior to normalizing the spectra, the noise levels were corrected to account for the losses through the boundary-layer Kevlar cloth as explained in the appendix. The frequency was scaled using the Strouhal number with the chord as the length scale ($St = fC/U_\infty$ with C=chord and U_∞ = free-stream velocity).

172

The complete set of maps was visually inspected to identify configurations showing the presence of trailing-edge noise. In the integrated spectrum, results are presented for only the one-twelfth frequency bands that show trailing-edge noise.

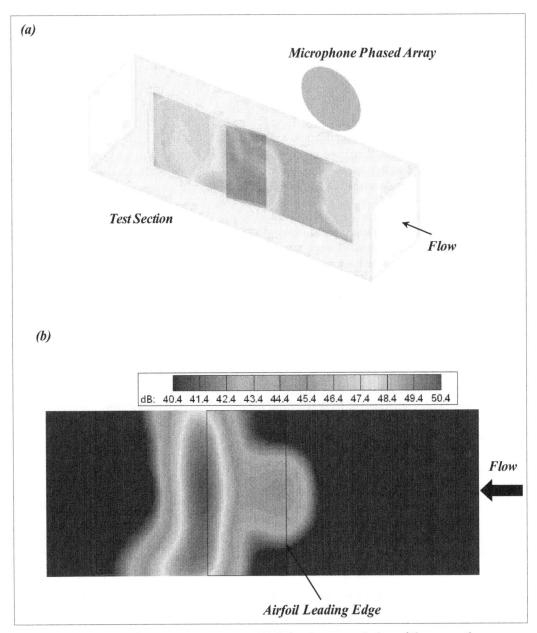

Figure 165 (a) Beamforming measurement plane for the computation of the acoustic maps; (b) typical acoustic map and color scale for airfoil noise level

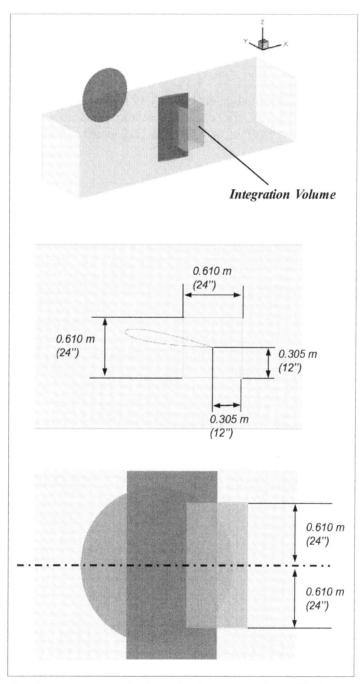

Figure 166. Beamforming measurement volume for the computation of the integrated spectrum to estimate trailing-edge noise

The following subsections present the results for the empty tunnel and the airfoils. The test matrices for the microphone phased array measurements are shown in Table 9 through Table 14

174

for the empty tunnel, small (0.2-m chord) NACA 0012, large chord NACA 0012, DU96, B1-18, and S831 airfoils, respectively. These tables list all of the configurations tested, the tunnel flow speed, the effective angle of attack, and the tunnel condition, such as fan speed (rpm) and tunnel temperature. The effective angle of attack was estimated from the pressure distribution discussed in Section 3 (above).

The reason for including results for the small NACA 0012 is that testing of a similar size NACA airfoil has been conducted in the past in an open-jet anechoic tunnel (Brooks et al. 1989). This allows for a preliminary validation of the new Virginia Tech tunnel to previously accepted data from an open-jet anechoic facility.

4.4. Empty-Tunnel Results

The empty-tunnel noise was measured for both tunnel entries as shown in Table 9. The one-twelfth octave band average noise spectra of the empty tunnel at 28 m/s, 42 m/s, and 54 m/s for both tunnel entries are shown in Figure 167(a). The data from both entries agree well, in particular considering the significant difference in tunnel temperature. The empty-tunnel spectrum essentially is broadband, but several tones are observed, in particular below 900 Hz.

The July empty-tunnel spectra then were scaled by the sixth power of the flow velocity and shown in Figure 167(b). The noise spectra scale well with the sixth-power law. Scaling with respect to the fan speed leads to the same results, e.g. fan and flow speed for the empty tunnel are linear. It is important to note that the empty-tunnel noise spectra are not a true indication of the background noise with the model installed. The models produce blockage, therefore the tunnel fan must operate faster and, consequently, the background noise is louder than that measured with the empty tunnel. The fan speed operates at 459 rpm to achieve a 57 m/s flow speed (run 160 in Table 9), for example, and must run at 595 rpm when the S831 airfoil is installed at an effective angle of attack of 6° for a flow speed of 56.47 m/s (run 150 in Table 14).

Table 9. Test Matrix for Microphone Phased Array Measurements of Empty Tunnel

Airfoil Configuration	Effective AoA (deg)	Trip	Flow Speed (m/s)	Fan Speed (rpm)	Tunnel Temp. (°F)	Run Number	Date
Empty tunnel	N/A	N/A	16	139	27.7	155	7/27/2007
Empty tunnel	N/A	N/A	20	180	27.7	156	7/27/2007
Empty tunnel	N/A	N/A	28	235	27.6	157	7/27/2007
Empty tunnel	N/A	N/A	40	335	27.6	158	7/27/2007
Empty tunnel	N/A	N/A	50	416	27.4	159	7/27/2007
Empty tunnel	N/A	N/A	56	459	27.3	160	7/27/2007
Empty tunnel	N/A	N/A	57	469	27.3	161	7/27/2007
Empty tunnel	N/A	N/A	28	233	64.7	112	11/2007
Empty tunnel	N/A	N/A	42	343	65.3	113	11/2007
Empty tunnel	N/A	N/A	54	432	67.7	114	11/2007

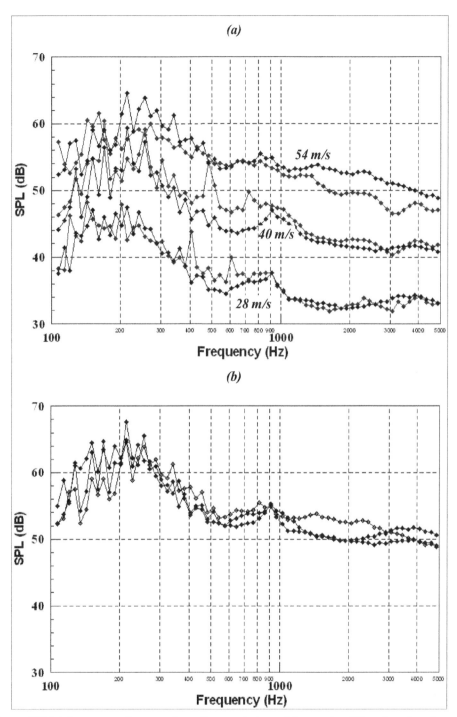

Figure 167 (a) Average noise spectrum for empty tunnel in one-twelfth octave bands; and (b) levels normalized using the sixth power of the flow velocity; tunnel entry: July 2007 (black), November-December (blue) 2007

4.5. Airfoil Results

This section presents the results for the tested airfoils. The data in this section consist of the integrated spectra and selected acoustic maps in one-twelfth octave bands.

4.5.1. Small Chord NACA 0012 Airfoil

Table 10 shows the test matrix for this airfoil. Measurements were performed for 42 m/s and 54 m/s flow speeds corresponding to nominal chord Reynolds number of 500,000 and 625,000. The boundary layer was tripped from the leading edge to 20%-chord. The acoustic maps show an extremely clear noise source at the trailing edge of the airfoil at virtually all of the one-twelfth octave bands from 500 Hz to 5,000 Hz.

Figure 168 shows the integrated spectra for both tripped and no-trip conditions. To aid in the visualization of the results, the data for the tripped airfoil cases are presented in red. The integration volume is very similar to that used for the large models (*see* Figure 166). It extends along the same two-thirds spanwise direction of the airfoil length but the cross section is smaller (0.15 m × 0.15 m). The untripped conditions show vortex shedding at all angles of attack tested. Based on a comparison to a similar airfoil measured by Brooks et al. (1989), the noise source mechanism is identified as laminar-boundary-layer vortex shedding. The vortex shedding frequencies match very closely the data shown by Brooks et al. (1989). These frequencies also collapse very well with the Strouhal number as shown in Figure 205. Noise maps at the peak of the vortex shedding are also included in Figure 168 (flow is from right to left). The maps clearly shows two distinct noise sources near the airfoil mid-span at the trailing edge. The results indicate the tripping of the boundary layer to be very effective at eliminating the clear vortex shedding. The noise spectra for the tripped airfoils for different angles of attack are virtually undistinguishable. As shown in Figures 205 and 206, the levels follow the fifth power law well for both untripped and tripped conditions.

Table 10. Test Matrix for Microphone Phased-Array Measurements of Small NACA 0012 Airfoil

Airfoil Configuration	Effective AoA (deg)	Trip	Flow Speed (m/s)	Fan Speed (rpm)	Tunnel Temp. (°F)	Run Number	Date
Small NACA 0012	0	No trip	43.46	383	99.4	64	7/9/2007
Small NACA 0012	0	No trip	43.13	383	98.5	65	7/9/2007
Small NACA 0012	0	No trip	54.67	482	98.7	66	7/9/2007
Small NACA 0012	3.1	No trip	43.54	382	100	62	7/9/2007
Small NACA 0012	3.1	No trip	54.92	480	101	63	7/9/2007
Small NACA 0012	7.3	No trip	41.49	350	85.5	80	7/10/2007
Small NACA 0012	7.3	No trip	52.21	350	86	81	7/10/2007
Small NACA 0012	0	Tripped	40.31	334	76.7	67	7/10/2007
Small NACA 0012	0	Tripped	50.89	420	78.1	68	7/10/2007
Small NACA 0012	0	Tripped	40.48	337	78.1	69	7/10/2007
Small NACA 0012	0	Tripped	51.04	423	79.3	70	7/10/2007
Small NACA 0012	2	Tripped	40.63	341	79.2	71	7/10/2007
Small NACA 0012	2	Tripped	40.63	341	79.2	72	7/10/2007
Small NACA 0012	2	Tripped	51.40	428	81.1	73	7/10/2007
Small NACA 0012	4	Tripped	40.94	343	81.4	74	7/10/2007
Small NACA 0012	4	Tripped	51.59	429	82.4	75	7/10/2007
Small NACA 0012	5.3	Tripped	41.11	345	83	76	7/10/2007
Small NACA 0012	5.3	Tripped	52.02	435	84.8	77	7/10/2007

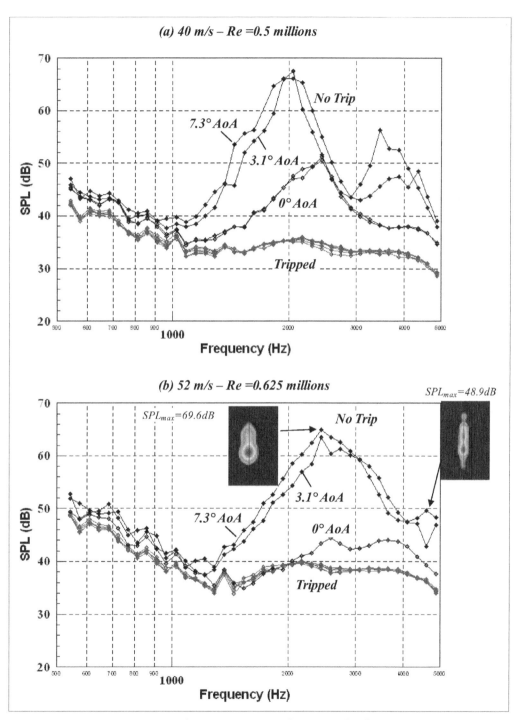

Figure 168. Integrated spectrum for 0.2-m chord NACA0012 airfoil for both tripped and no-trip conditions at nominal chord Reynolds numbers (a) 500,000 and (b) 625,000

To gain confidence in the trailing-edge measurements in this new facility, the results for this small NACA 0012 airfoil were compared to the data reported by Brooks et al. (1989). For a valid comparison, the Virginia Tech integrated spectrum had to be corrected to put the results in the same basis as in the work by Brooks et al. (1989). Thus, the integrated spectrum was corrected for losses through the Kevlar window, the shear layer, distance to the model, model span, and levels adjusted from one-twelfth to one-third octave bands. Figure 169 compares trailing-edge noise measured by Brooks et al. (1989) for a 22.86-cm-chord airfoil (solid line) and measured in the VT Stability Wind Tunnel for a 20-cm-chord airfoil, at angle of attack of 0° and 5.3° (red symbols). The flow speeds in the open-jet and VT wind tunnels were 40 m/s and 40.5 m/s, respectively. Results obtained in the VT wind tunnel are in good agreement with those obtained by Brooks et al. (1989), particularly in the 1,000 Hz to 4,000 Hz range. However, differences of up to about 6 dB are observed below 1,000 Hz. Considering that the tests were conducted in different wind tunnel facilities and using different methods to compute the airfoil self-noise, the comparison can be considered acceptable and provides a first validation of the facility. For the sake of completeness, Figure 170 shows the noise maps for 5.3° angle of attack at 40 m/s for the tripped condition in one-third octave bands. For frequencies of less than 1,000 Hz, beamforming maps are dominated by strong noise sources at the junction of the airfoil with the test-section floor and ceiling. The volume used to compute the integrated spectra excludes the junction region so these junction sources are not included in the computation of the trailing-edge noise. Results for frequencies greater than 4,000 Hz are not reliable due to the large size of the array and because the array was not calibrated for phase.

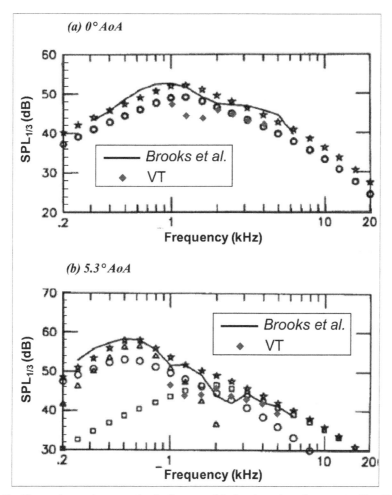

Figure 169. Trailing-edge noise spectra in the one-third octave band measured by Brooks et al. (solid black lines) in an open-jet wind tunnel for a 22.86-cm-chord airfoil in flow with a speed of 39.6 m/s and measured in the VT Stability Wind Tunnel for a 20-cm-chord airfoil (red solid dots) in a flow with a speed of 40.5 m/s, at angles of attack of (a) 0° and (b) 5.3°

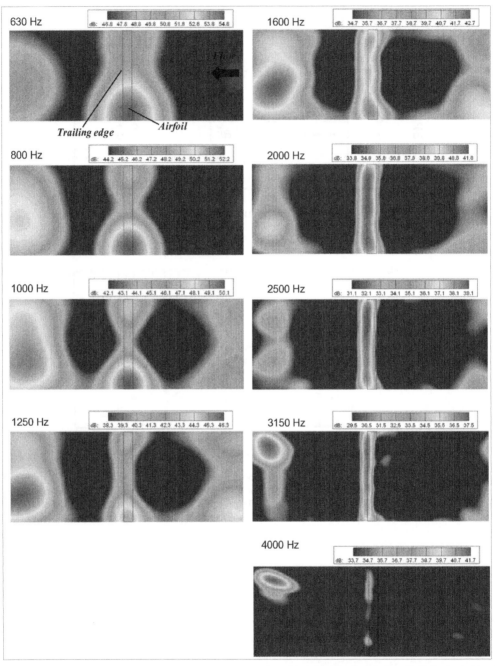

Figure 170. Acoustic maps for tripped small 0.2-m chord NACA 0012 airfoil at 5.3° AoA at 40 m/s flow speed (Re = 500,000); acoustic maps are in one-third octave bands

4.5.2. NACA 0012 Airfoil

The test matrix for this model is provided in Table 11. The NACA 0012 was tested extensively in both tunnel entries. During the July tunnel entry, the airfoil was tested at small effective angles of attack (0° to 4°), for a broad range of flow speeds (nominal chord Reynolds numbers from 800,000 to 3,800,000), and for both tripped and untripped conditions. The November-December entry focused on a wider range of angle of attack (from 14° to -14° in steps of 2°) and 3 flow speeds (nominal chord Reynolds number 1,500,000; 2,200,000; and 3,200,000) mainly for clean configurations (no trip).

Trailing-edge noise was measured successfully for nearly all of the configurations at effective angles of attack of ±10° and smaller, and at most of the one-twelfth octave bands. Figure 171 through Figure 174 illustrate the 38 one-twelfth octave band acoustic maps for the case of untripped 4° angle of attack at 28.5 m/s (Re = 1,500,000). The plots show the flow from right to left, and each plot has its own scale. The maps use rectangles to indicate the airfoils, and show the one-twelfth octave center frequency in the top-left corner. This case was selected because it clearly shows trailing-edge noise in most of the frequency bands, for example for the 542-Hz through 3,649-Hz bands (except for the 3,251-Hz band).

Table 11. Test Matrix for Microphone Phased Array Measurements of NACA 0012 Airfoil

Airfoil Configuration	Effective AoA (deg)	Trip	Flow Speed (m/s)	Fan Speed (rpm)	Tunnel Temp. (°F)	Run Number	Date
NACA 0012	-14	No trip	28.53	274	68.1	107	12/10/2007
NACA 0012	-14	No trip	42.28	404	67.8	108	12/10/2007
NACA 0012	-14	No trip	54.59	523	70	109	12/10/2007
NACA 0012	-14	No trip	54.14	518	69.2	110	12/10/2007
NACA 0012	-12	No trip	28.25	265	66.4	104	12/10/2007
NACA 0012	-12	No trip	42.35	397	66.9	105	12/10/2007
NACA 0012	-12	No trip	54.09	507	68.7	106	12/10/2007
NACA 0012	-10	No trip	28.39	261	65.8	101	12/10/2007
NACA 0012	-10	No trip	42.20	386	65.9	102	12/10/2007
NACA 0012	-10	No trip	54.01	491	67.1	103	12/10/2007
NACA 0012	-8	No trip	28.16	252	65.9	95	12/10/2007
NACA 0012	-8	No trip	42.61	376	65.5	96	12/10/2007
NACA 0012	-8	No trip	54.03	475	67.1	97	12/10/2007
NACA 0012	-6	No trip	28.29	246	65.1	92	12/10/2007
NACA 0012	-6	No trip	42.27	363	64.9	93	12/10/2007
NACA 0012	-6	No trip	53.97	460	66.1	94	12/10/2007
NACA 0012	-4	No trip	28.84	247	65.1	89	12/10/2007
NACA 0012	-4	No trip	42.47	358	64.6	90	12/10/2007
NACA 0012	-4	No trip	53.62	445	65.7	91	12/10/2007
NACA 0012	-2	No trip	28.84	240	65.3	86	12/10/2007
NACA 0012	-2	No trip	42.53	356	64.8	87	12/10/2007
NACA 0012	-2	No trip	53.96	447	65.9	88	12/10/2007
NACA 0012	0	No trip	16.01	140	84.6	30	7/3/2007
NACA 0012	0	No trip	20.09	177	85.8	31	7/3/2007
NACA 0012	0	No trip	28.05	245	90.2	32	7/3/2007
NACA 0012	0	No trip	30.02	258	91.1	33	7/3/2007
NACA 0012	0	No trip	40.15	340	92.2	34	7/3/2007

Airfoil Configuration	Effective AoA (deg)	Trip	Flow Speed (m/s)	Fan Speed (rpm)	Tunnel Temp. (°F)	Run Number	Date
NACA 0012	0	No trip	50.08	431	92.4	35	7/3/2007
NACA 0012	0	No trip	58.07	491	93	36	7/3/2007
NACA 0012	0	No trip	60.11	504	94.4	37	7/3/2007
NACA 0012	0	No trip	66.45	560	95	38	7/3/2007
NACA 0012	0	No trip	28.39	238	68	62	12/10/2007
NACA 0012	0	No trip	42.33	349	68.5	63	12/10/2007
NACA 0012	0	No trip	54.09	439	69.7	64	12/10/2007
NACA 0012	2	No trip	28.51	239	69.5	65	12/10/2007
NACA 0012	2	No trip	42.48	355	69.7	66	12/10/2007
NACA 0012	2	No trip	54.28	455	70.7	67	12/10/2007
NACA 0012	2	No trip	15.29	138	74.4	58	7/3/2007
NACA 0012	2	No trip	19.78	177	74.4	59	7/3/2007
NACA 0012	2	No trip	27.84	245	74.3	60	7/3/2007
NACA 0012	4	No trip	28.52	244	70	68	12/10/2007
NACA 0012	4	No trip	42.39	359	70.1	69	12/10/2007
NACA 0012	4	No trip	54.53	461	71.5	70	12/10/2007
NACA 0012	6	No trip	28.62	252	71	71	12/10/2007
NACA 0012	6	No trip	42.43	371	71.1	72	12/10/2007
NACA 0012	6	No trip	54.32	472	72.4	73	12/10/2007
NACA 0012	8	No trip	28.55	259	71.3	74	12/10/2007
NACA 0012	8	No trip	42.46	382	71.7	75	12/10/2007
NACA 0012	8	No trip	54.34	492	72.7	76	12/10/2007
NACA 0012	8	No trip	27.84	275	74.4	61	7/3/2007
NACA 0012	10	No trip	28.48	263	71.7	77	12/10/2007
NACA 0012	10	No trip	42.47	396	72	78	12/10/2007
NACA 0012	10	No trip	54.38	510	73.8	79	12/10/2007
NACA 0012	14	No trip	28.41	283	69.4	80	12/10/2007
NACA 0012	14	No trip	42.49	420	70	81	12/10/2007
NACA 0012	14	No trip	54.30	538	72.2	82	12/10/2007
NACA 0012	12	No trip	28.31	270	62.9	83	12/10/2007
NACA 0012	12	No trip	42.12	410	63.6	84	12/10/2007
NACA 0012	12	No trip	53.77	521	66.1	85	12/10/2007
NACA 0012	0	Tripped	10.40	97	99	39	7/3/2007
NACA 0012	0	Tripped	16.24	145	99.7	40	7/3/2007
NACA 0012	0	Tripped	20.36	177	99.6	41	7/3/2007
NACA 0012	0	Tripped	28.07	240	99.4	42	7/3/2007
NACA 0012	0	Tripped	30.02	258	98.8	43	7/3/2007
NACA 0012	0	Tripped	40.06	342	97.1	44	7/3/2007
NACA 0012	0	Tripped	50.02	415	96.6	45	7/3/2007
NACA 0012	0	Tripped	58.03	469	94	46	7/3/2007
NACA 0012	0	Tripped	60.06	479	94.5	47	7/3/2007
NACA 0012	0	Tripped	66.57	526	94.5	48	7/3/2007
NACA 0012	2	Tripped	27.94	246	75.1	57	7/3/2007
NACA 0012	2	Tripped	16.09	105	89.1	49	7/3/2007
NACA 0012	2	Tripped	20.86	193	90	50	7/3/2007
NACA 0012	4	Tripped	15.48	143	77.3	51	7/3/2007
NACA 0012	4	Tripped	19.96	184	78.6	52	7/3/2007

183

Airfoil Configuration	Effective AoA (deg)	Trip	Flow Speed (m/s)	Fan Speed (rpm)	Tunnel Temp. (°F)	Run Number	Date
NACA 0012	4	Tripped	28.07	257	77	53	7/3/2007
NACA 0012	5.3	Tripped	15.45	146	75.8	54	7/3/2007
NACA 0012	5.3	Tripped	19.81	186	75.7	55	7/3/2007
NACA 0012	5.3	Tripped	27.97	262	75.9	56	7/3/2007
NACA 0012	-8	Tripped	28.13	253	64.8	98	12/10/2007
NACA 0012	-8	Tripped	42.38	376	65	99	12/10/2007
NACA 0012	-8	Tripped	53.87	475	66.6	100	12/10/2007

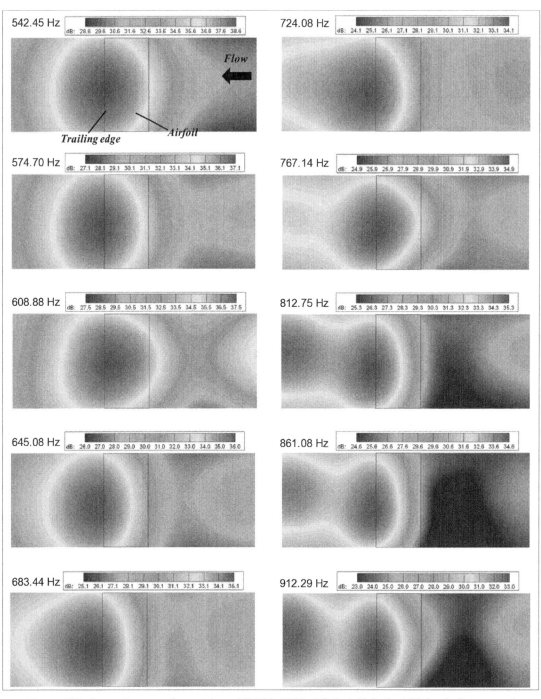

Figure 171. Acoustic maps for untripped NACA 0012 airfoil at 4° AoA at 28.5 m/s flow speed (scale: one-twelfth octave bands)

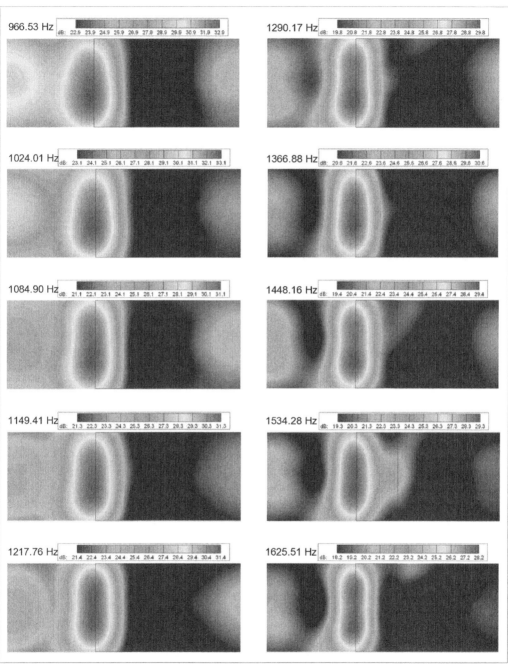

Figure 172. Acoustic maps for untripped NACA 0012 airfoil at 4° AoA at 28.5 m/s flow speed
(scale: one-twelfth octave bands)

186

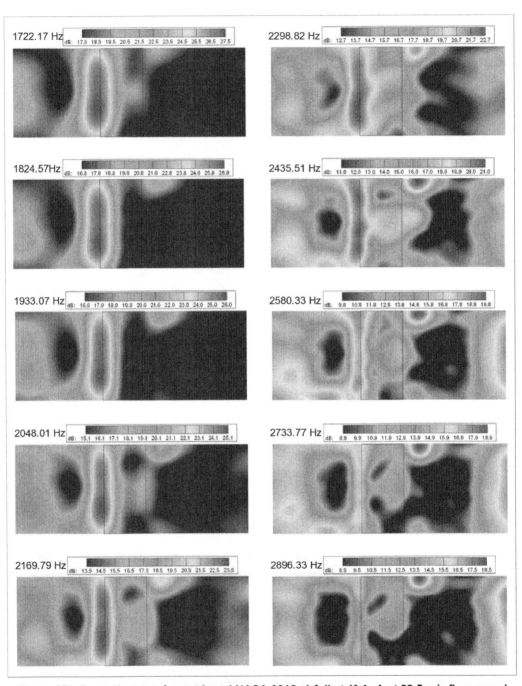

Figure 173. Acoustic maps for untripped NACA 0012 airfoil at 4° AoA at 28.5 m/s flow speed (scale: one-twelfth octave bands)

187

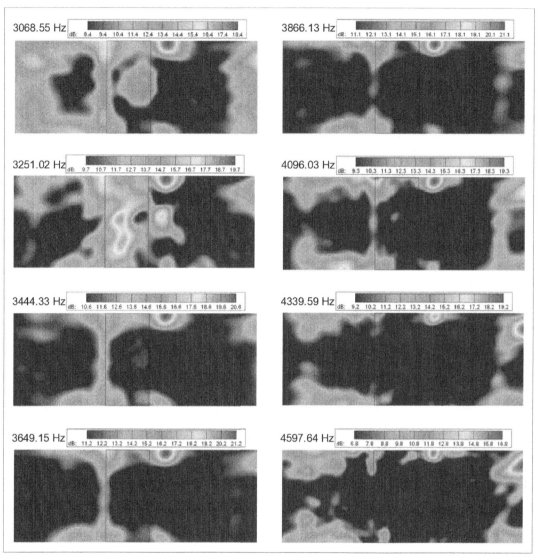

Figure 174. Acoustic maps for untripped NACA 0012 airfoil at 4° AoA at 28.5 m/s flow speed (scale: one-twelfth octave bands)

In terms of the angle of attack, the NACA 0012 airfoil shows a clear demarcation in its behavior. Namely, at all flow speeds vortex shedding takes place for angles of attack that are equal to or greater than 6°. Figure 175 shows the integrated spectra for 0°, 2°, and 4° angles of attack at flow velocities of 28 m/s, 42 m/s, and 54 m/s. This plot shows the trailing-edge noise as a relatively flat spectrum that rolls off at a particular flow-dependent frequency.

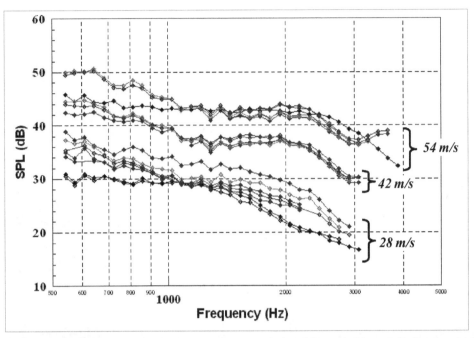

Figure 175. Integrated spectrum for untripped NACA 0012 airfoil at 0°, 2°, and 4°effective AoA for 28 m/s, 42m/s, and 54 m/s; nominal chord Reynolds number from 1,500,000 to 3,200,000 (scale: one-twelfth octave bands); tunnel entry data for July 2007 (black) and November-December 2007 data (blue and green)

The results are also plotted in more detail in Figure 176 through Figure 186. These figures show the integrated spectra for the cases of untripped airfoil for effective angles of attack of 0°, 2°, 4°, 6°, 8°, and 10°. Results are shown for nominal chord Reynolds numbers of from 800,000 to 3,200,000. Figure 176 and Figure 177 for 0° and 2° angles of attack show very similar results, an essentially flat spectrum that rolls off with a slope of approximate 10 dB per octave. A few acoustic maps also are supplied (flow is from right to left). The 2° angle of attack at the 28 m/s configuration was tested in both tunnel entries, thus enabling direct comparison of the same configuration tested five months apart. These two results are provided in Figure 177. They show very good agreement for the flat part of the spectrum, although they differ on the slope of the roll off. The acoustic maps for the same 1,084.9 Hz band from both tunnel entries also are included, and the maximum level is indicated. Note that the maximum level for the July map is 4.7 dB higher. To compare the two maps, reduce the levels in the July maps by 6 dB (due to the reflective surface of the spiral array used during the July tunnel entry). The actual difference in levels is only 1.3 dB; the integration gives virtually the same result. Figure 178 shows the case of ±4° angle of attack. The results for positive and negative angles of attack match relatively well, with some differences occurring at the lowest speed of 28 m/s. Also, the spectrum at this speed is not as flat as that of the smaller angles of attack. The normalized spectra in Figure 207 show that the fifth power law collapses the data very well for these configurations, in particular for 0° and 2° angles of attack.

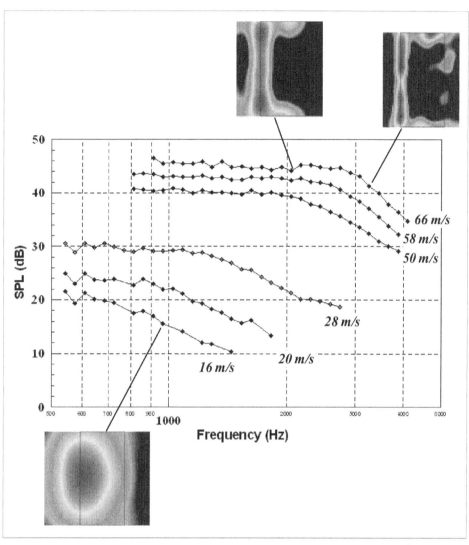

Figure 176. Integrated spectrum for untripped NACA 0012 airfoil at 0° effective AoA
(scale: one-twelfth octave bands); tunnel entry data for July 2007 (black)

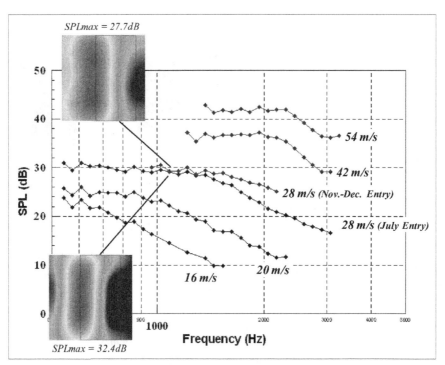

Figure 177. Integrated spectrum for untripped NACA 0012 airfoil at 2° effective AoA (scale: one-twelfth octave bands); tunnel entry data for July 2007 (black) and November-December 2007 (blue)

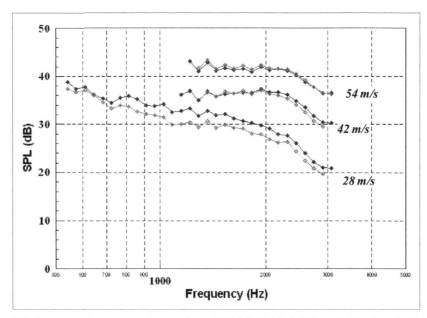

Figure 178. Integrated spectrum for untripped NACA 0012 airfoil at 4° (blue) and -4° (green) effective AoA (scale: one-twelfth octave bands; tunnel entry: November-December 2007)

The results for 6°, 8°, and 10° angles of attack shown in Figure 179 through Figure 181 differ from the previous results in that they clearly show vortex shedding from the trailing edge. For these cases both positive and negative angles were measured and, in general, shedding took place in all conditions except for the 8° and ±10° angles of attack at 28 m/s. The fundamental shedding frequency at the lowest flow speed of 28 m/s occurs at approximately 350 Hz and it therefore isn't shown in the integrated spectra (e.g., the first peak shown in Figure 179 and Figure 180 is the first harmonic). The existence of vortex shedding at high angles of attack and Reynolds numbers in the NACA0012 airfoil has been previously observed (Paterson et al. 1973). In this work, it was concluded that the presence of the vortex shedding was associated with a laminar boundary layer on the airfoil pressure surface. They also provided a scaling frequency law to estimate the vortex shedding frequency. Using this equation for the airfoil tested here predicts the vortex shedding to occur at 418 Hz, 768 Hz, and 1,120 Hz for 28 m/s, 40 m/s, and 52 m/s, respectively. These values agree well with the experimentally observed frequencies (e.g., 350 Hz, 650 Hz, 900 Hz). Also, the shedding frequency scales very well with the Strouhal number as shown in Figure 207. Therefore, laminar-boundary-layer-vortex shedding is the noise mechanism for the results in Figure 179 through Figure 181.

To provide further insight, these figures include selected acoustic maps. The acoustic images reveal that there are multiple noise sources at the trailing edge along the span radiating at slightly different frequencies. In Figure 181 (42 m/s), for example, the airfoil sheds vortices at 608 Hz from the upper part of the airfoil and shows a shedding frequency of 812 Hz from the lower section of the trailing edge. In fact, three distinct shedding frequencies are evident from different parts of the airfoil edge. Again the existence of multiple tones was also observed by Paterson et al. (1973). They concluded that these multiple frequencies were aerodynamic in nature. This observation of multiple frequencies is not surprising because the flow is three-dimensional; it is impossible to get a purely two-dimensional response at a single shedding frequency.

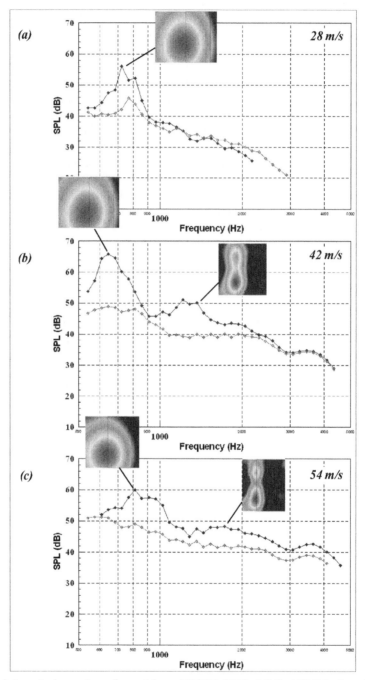

Figure 179. Integrated spectrum for untripped NACA 0012 airfoil at 6° (blue) and -6° (green) effective AoA (scale: one-twelfth octave bands; tunnel entry: November-December 2007)

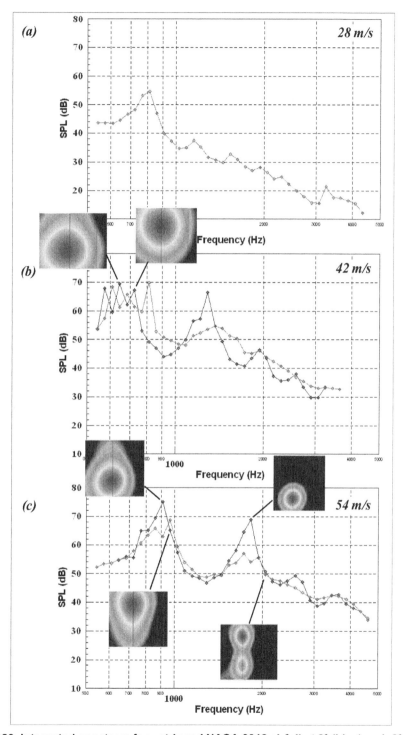

Figure 180. Integrated spectrum for untripped NACA 0012 airfoil at 8° (blue) and -8° (green) effective AoA (scale: one-twelfth octave bands; tunnel entry: November-December 2007)

194

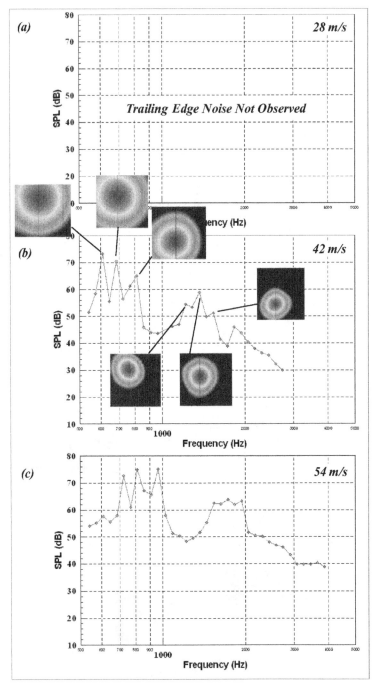

Figure 181. Integrated spectrum for untripped NACA 0012 airfoil at -10° (green) effective AoA (scale: one-twelfth octave bands; tunnel entry: November-December 2007); note that the trailing-edge noise for 10° AoA was not observed

At the greatest angles of ±12° and ±14°, there are strong noise sources at the junctions of the airfoil with the tunnel floor and ceiling on the leading edge. Additionally, there seems to be a noise source that is one-quarter chord downstream from the leading edge of the airfoil—suggesting a potential flow irregularity, such as unsteady laminar-to-turbulence boundary transition or a separation bubble. These noise sources, particularly at the junctions, hide noise from the trailing edge. Figure 182 illustrates this behavior in a few selected maps for ±12° effective angle of attack at 28.3 m/s flow speed.

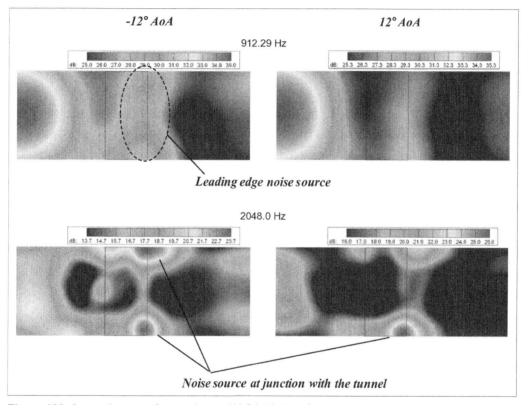

Figure 182. Acoustic maps for untripped NACA 0012 airfoil at -12° and 12° AoA at 28.3 m/s flow speed (scale: one-twelfth octave bands; tunnel entry: November-December 2007)

The effect of tripping the airfoil is evaluated in Figure 183 through Figure 186. The data for the tripped airfoil cases are presented in red. The corresponding untripped data also are plotted in the same figures (most is shown above in Figure 175 through Figure 181). Figure 183 shows the case of 0° angle of attack for flow speeds ranging from 16 m/s to 66 m/s (Re from 800,000 to 3,800,000). Tripping the boundary layer leads to trailing-edge noise reduction mainly in the roll off portion of the spectrum. Noise attenuations are in the 2 dB to 3 dB range, with the better results at the lower Reynolds numbers. The acoustic maps for the 1,722.17 Hz band at 28 m/s illustrate the trailing-edge noise reduction. The maximum levels in these maps also are indicated because they are not the same. The levels are very similar (25.1 dB to 24.5 dB), however, and enable a direct visual comparison of the maps.

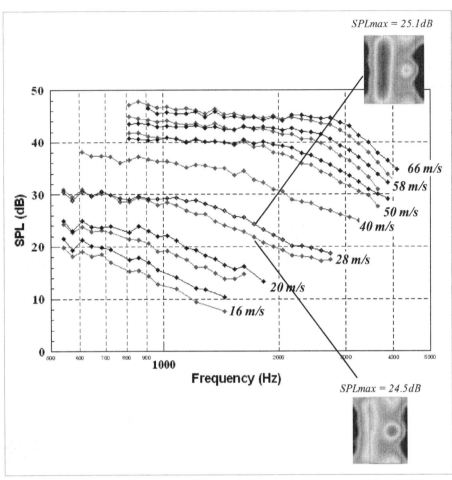

Figure 183. Integrated spectrum for untripped (black) and tripped (red) NACA 0012 airfoil at 0° effective AoA (scale: one-twelfth octave bands; tunnel entry: July 2007)

Figure 184 shows the same results for 2° angle of attack at 16 m/s, 20 m/s, and 28 m/s (higher Reynolds numbers were not measured). Tripping is more effective for this angle of attack with a maximum noise reduction of approximately 5 dB. The attenuation, however, again mostly is in the roll-off section of the spectrum. Tripping for the 4° angle of attack case can be evaluated only for the flow speed of 28 m/s (e.g. run 68 from the November-December versus run 53 from July). This comparison is shown in Figure 185, which also includes data from untripped airfoil at 42 m/s and 54 m/s as well as from the tripped airfoil at 16 m/s and 20 m/s. The noise reduction is significant, ranging from 5 dB at low frequency to 18 dB at 2,000 Hz. Unlike the results in Figure 183 and Figure 184, the reduction in Figure 185 is based on comparing data that were measured 5 months apart. Comparing the results for 28 m/s in Figure 183 through Figure 185, there is a clear increase in the reduction due to tripping with increasing angles of attack. However, it is likely that the attenuation at 4° is overestimated.

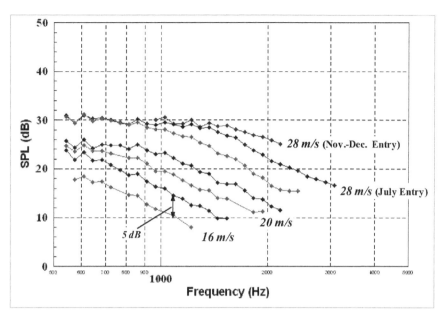

Figure 184. Integrated spectrum for untripped (black and blue) and tripped (red) NACA 0012 airfoil at 2° effective AoA (scale: one-twelfth octave bands; tunnel entry: July (black and red) and November-December (blue) 2007)

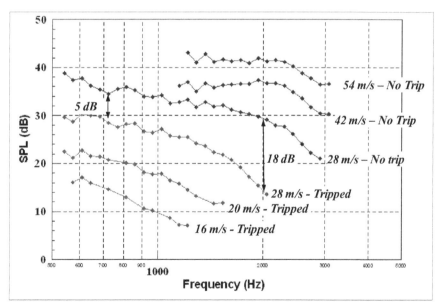

Figure 185. Integrated spectrum for untripped (blue) and tripped (red) NACA 0012 airfoil at 4° effective AoA (scale: one-twelfth octave bands; tunnel entry: July (red), November-December (blue) 2007)

198

The effect of tripping for higher angles of attack can be evaluated for the case of -8° angle of attack for 28 m/s, 42 m/s, and 54 m/s flow speeds as shown in Figure 186. For this configuration the noise from the clean (no trip) airfoil is dominated by vortex shedding at distinct frequencies. Tripping the boundary layer leads to significant reduction of some of the shedding (and thus attenuation of noise), in particular at 42 m/s and 54 m/s (Figure 186(b), (c)). Not all the shedding is reduced, however. In Figure 186(b), for example, the shedding in the 608 Hz band clearly is reduced (but not eliminated completely). The shedding occurring in the 812 Hz band is virtually unaffected. Additional insight can be gained by revisiting the work of Paterson et al. (1973). They found that the only effective location for the trip to eliminate the vortex shedding was forward of 80% chord on the pressure surface. This result confirms that lack of effectiveness of the trip used in the experiments here. Furthermore, it also confirms that the noise source is laminar-boundary-layer-vortex shedding. As shown in Appendix C, the tripped cases scale well with the fifth power of the free-stream velocity, in particular for the lower angles of attack where vortex shedding doesn't take place.

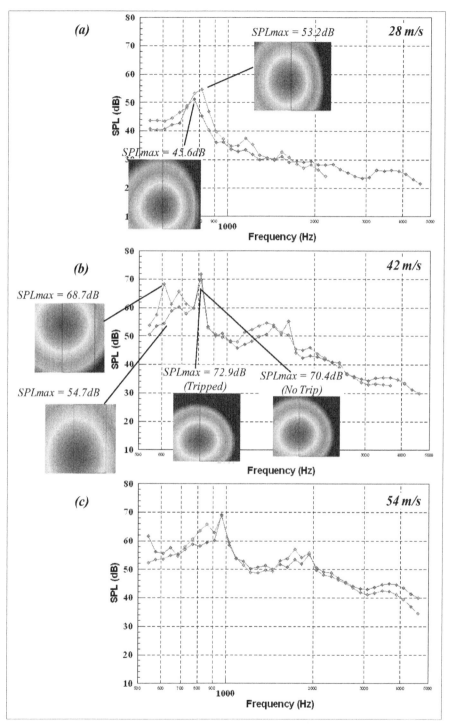

Figure 186. Integrated spectrum for untripped (green) versus tripped (red) NACA 0012 airfoil at -8° effective AoA (scale: one-twelfth octave bands; tunnel entry: November-December 2007)

4.5.3. Delft DU96 Airfoil

The test matrix for the DU96 airfoil is shown in Table 12. Most of the test configurations (27 out of 33) were measured during the July tunnel entry. Unfortunately, the 6 cases tested during the November-December entry did not show trailing-edge noise except at a very few low-frequency bands. The results from the first entry are presented here. Airfoil data are available for 3 Reynolds numbers (1,500,000, 2,500,000, 3,200,000) and angles of attack of 3°, 6°, 7°, 8°, and 10° for the untripped condition. Trailing-edge noise was not clearly observed at the highest angle of attack tested (12°) at 54 m/s flow speed. More specifically, strong noise sources were observed at the junction of the model and test section (both at the leading and trailing edges) as well as other extraneous sources in the test section. Therefore, care must be exercised for interpretation of the 12° results. It should also be noted that the airfoil probably stalls at this angle (see the pressure data shown in Figure 75) and it is possible that separation-stall noise dominates. Additionally, selected cases were tested tripping the boundary layer, and only a single soiled case was tested.

Table 12. Test Matrix for Microphone Phased Array Measurements of DU96 Airfoil

Airfoil Configuration	Effective AoA (deg)	Trip	Flow Speed (m/s)	Fan Speed (rpm)	Tunnel Temp. (°F)	Run Number	Date
DU96	1	No trip	27	231	50.4	48	11/30/2007
DU96	3	No trip	26	238	52.1	49	11/30/2007
DU96	3	No trip	29	276	80.1	102	7/17/2007
DU96	3	No trip	41	417	106.3	117	7/19/2007
DU96	3	No trip	59	598	107.2	118	7/19/2007
DU96	6	No trip	29	297	84.2	103	7/17/2007
DU96	6	No trip	41	433	105.8	119	7/19/2007
DU96	6	No trip	59	621	108.3	120	7/19/2007
DU96	7	No trip	41	440	106.6	121	7/19/2007
DU96	7	No trip	59	629	109.6	122	7/19/2007
DU96	7	No trip	29	302	85.1	104	7/17/2007
DU96	7	No trip	29	292	85.6	127	7/20/2007
DU96	7	No trip	58	609	85.6	128	7/20/2007
DU96	8	No trip	41	445	106.4	123	7/19/2007
DU96	8	No trip	59	638	110.5	124	7/19/2007
DU96	8	No trip	29	305	86.7	105	7/17/2007
DU96	8	No trip	27	259	53.4	50	11/30/2007
DU96	8	No trip	54	522	57.7	51	11/30/2007
DU96	8	No trip	55	525	61.3	52[1]	11/30/2007
DU96	10	No trip	30	313	90.0	106	7/17/2007
DU96	10	No trip	41	452	107.0	125	7/19/2007
DU96	10	No trip	59	645	110.2	126	7/19/2007
DU96	12	No trip	55	538	64.0	53	11/30/2007
DU96	3	Tripped	29	268	77.8	108	7/18/2007
DU96	3	Tripped	41	413	104.0	115	7/19/2007
DU96	3	Tripped	58	597	106.8	116	7/19/2007
DU96	3	Tripped	57	510	78.6	109	7/19/2007
DU96	7	Tripped	28	281	75.7	107	7/18/2007
DU96	7	Tripped	58	631	103.4	113	7/19/2007
DU96	7	Tripped	40	437	90.0	114	7/19/2007

Airfoil Configuration	Effective AoA (deg)	Trip	Flow Speed (m/s)	Fan Speed (rpm)	Tunnel Temp. (°F)	Run Number	Date
DU96	10	Tripped	57	601	80.0	110	7/19/2007
DU96	10	Tripped	57	603	88.0	111	7/19/2007
DU96	10	Soiled	58	565	100.1	154	7/26/2007
Note that the data were not saved.							

Figure 187 shows the trailing-edge noise for all clean conditions (no trip) for the three flow speeds at angles of attack of 3° through 10°. The case of 12° AoA at 54 m/s was also included (blue curve). Note that—in many cases—at the higher speed, trailing-edge noise was difficult to observe from the noise maps. Therefore results greater than 1,000 Hz for 42 m/s and 54 m/s should be regarded as preliminary. A few illustrative noise maps are also shown. The data show a very weak dependence of the noise levels on the angle of attack for all three speeds. In fact, the data are within a range of about 2 dB and thus no obvious trend can be concluded. The noise maps for the 574 Hz band show the noise source located at the trailing edge as the result of the scattering of the turbulence with the trailing edge, e.g. turbulence-boundary-layer-trailing-edge noise. On the other hand, the spectrum for the 12° angle of attack shows a noticeable increase. Moreover, the acoustic map for the 2,435 Hz band reveals a dominant source on the lower half of the airfoil. It is interesting that the source is slightly downstream from the trailing edge. This likely is an indication of separation-stall noise. Similar behavior is discussed for the B1-18 airfoil later.

To assess the effect of tripping the boundary layer, the data for tripped cases are superimposed with the clean conditions in Figure 188. Again the data shows virtually no clear angle of attack effect on the tripped cases (shown in red). There is a noticeable reduction in the noise, however, for the tripped condition at the lowest speed. The reduction ranges from 2 dB at low frequency to about 5 dB at 2,000 Hz. The normalized spectra are shown in Figures 209 and 210. It again shows a good collapse of the data with the fifth power law.

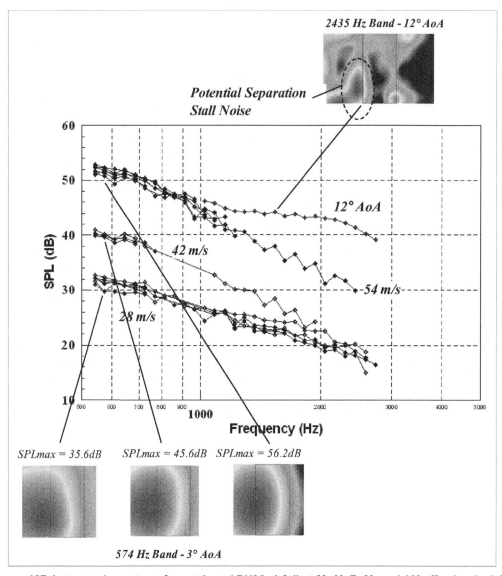

Figure 187. Integrated spectrum for untripped DU96 airfoil at 3°, 6°, 7, 8°, and 10° effective AoA for 28 m/s, 42 m/s, and 54 m/s (nominal chord Reynolds number: 1,500,000–3,200,000). Single result for 12° effective AoA is for 54 m/s (blue). (scale: one-twelfth octave bands; tunnel entry: July 2007)

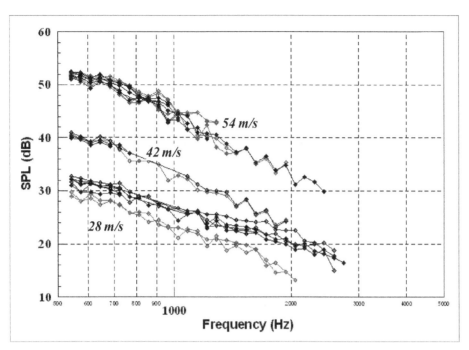

Figure 188. Integrated spectrum for untripped (black) and tripped (red) DU96 airfoil at 3°, 6°, 7°, 8°, and 10° effective AoA for 28 m/s, 42 m/s, and 54 m/s (nominal chord Reynolds number: 1,500,000–3,200,000) (scale: one-twelfth octave bands; tunnel entry: July 2007)

4.5.4. Risø B1-18 Airfoil

The test matrix for the B1-18 airfoil is shown in Table 13. As was the case for the DU96 airfoil, most of the test configurations were measured during the July tunnel entry. Data were collected for two flow speeds (28 m/s, 54 m/s), effective angles of attack from -4° (zero lift) to 13° (stall), and both clean and tripped boundary-layer conditions. Figures 189 through 191 show the noise spectrum for all the untripped cases for both speeds (including only data at the frequency bands where trailing-edge noise was identified in the acoustic maps). Figure 190 presents the spectra for angles of attack ranging between 3° and 13°. To better illustrate the dependence of the noise with the angle of attack, the results are presented for small (3° through 8°) and large (8° and 13°) angles separately. As a reference, the 8° case is shown in both plots. The results in Figure 190(a) show that trailing-edge noise decreases at higher frequencies (≥ 1,000 Hz) as the angle of attack increases from 3° to 8°. The noise levels remain virtually unchanged at the lower frequencies. As shown in Figure 190(b), this trend is reversed as the angle of attack goes beyond 8°. There is a noticeable increase in levels of the whole spectrum at the greatest angle of 13°. In Figure 190, the same behavior is observed when the angle of attack is increased from -4° to 3° without noticeable changes below 1,000 Hz. Note that reliable data for 6°, 7°, and 8° angles of attack extend from 500 Hz to just slightly above 1,000 Hz. Once again for the 11° and 13° angles of attack, a significant increase of the levels is observed (e.g., 8-10 dB). This behavior likely is due to potential flow separation as suggested by the mean-pressure distribution results (*see* Section 3) (e.g., separation stall noise). It was found that at the greater Reynolds number the flow over the suction side appeared almost completely stalled at 13° (*see* Figure 57). The pressure data indicate that the same separation behavior also seems to have occurred at the lower Reynolds number.

This flow separation could explain the jump in the spectrum at 28 m/s (Figure 189(b)). To gain further insight, acoustic maps at the 2,048 Hz and 3,649 Hz bands are shown in Figure 190. Similar to the DU96 airfoil, it is evident that the dominant noise source is just downstream of the trailing edge. This source appears in the maps quite differently from those produced by the turbulent or laminar boundary layer trailing-edge noise where the source is exactly on the trailing edge. These maps provide additional evidence that the airfoil is stalled and the source is separation-stall noise.

Table 13. Test Matrix for Microphone Phased Array Measurements of Risø B1-18 Airfoil

Airfoil Configuration	Effective AoA (deg)	Trip	Flow Speed[1] (m/s)	Fan Speed (rpm)	Tunnel Temp. (°F)	Run Number	Date
Risø	-4.7	No trip	56	452	58.0	40	11/28/2007
Risø	-4	No trip	58	445	56.0	41	11/28/2007
Risø	3	No trip	-	-	60.0	133[1]	7/24/2007
Risø	3	No trip	56	561	63.0	134	7/24/2007
Risø	3	No trip	56	562	63.0	135	7/24/2007
Risø	3	No trip	28	283	71.9	92	7/13/2007
Risø	3	No trip	56	507	58.4	42[2]	11/28/2007
Risø	6	No trip	56	529	60.3	43	11/28/2007
Risø	6	No trip	28	300	71.9	93	7/13/2007
Risø	6	No trip	28	301	72.4	94	7/13/2007
Risø	6	No trip	56	585	64.0	136	7/24/2007
Risø	7	No trip	56	593	66.2	137	7/24/2007
Risø	7	No trip	28	307	73.0	95	7/13/2007
Risø	8	No trip	56	597	67.0	138	7/24/2007
Risø	8	No trip	56	602	67.9	139	7/24/2007
Risø	8	No trip	28	310	73.0	96	7/13/2007
Risø	10	No trip	28	315	73.0	97	7/13/2007
Risø	10	No trip	56	–	71.5	140[3]	7/24/2007
Risø	11	No trip	57	623	74.9	141	7/24/2007
Risø	11	No trip	57	623	74.4	142	7/24/2007
Risø	11	No trip	28	317	73.1	98	7/13/2007
Risø	11	No trip	56	545	61.8	44	11/28/2007
Risø	11	No trip	28	268	60.0	45	11/28/2007
Risø	13	No trip	56	544	58.3	46	11/28/2007
Risø	13	No trip	28	303	73.3	99	7/13/2007
Risø	-3	Tripped	56	499	71.2	129	7/23/2007
Risø	3	Tripped	58	589	95.1	131	7/23/2007
Risø	3	Tripped	30	297	87.7	100	7/16/2007
Risø	6	Tripped	56	529	59.6	47	11/28/2007
Risø	6	Tripped	30	317	87.5	101	7/16/2007
Risø	6	Tripped	57	601	91.6	132	7/23/2007
Risø	7	Tripped	58	594	102.3	130[4]	7/23/2007
Risø	6	Soiled	57	597	79.4	143	7/24/2007

NOTES
1. Flow speed data were not available.
2. Data were not saved.
3. Fan speed was not recorded.
4. Data file was corrupted and case could not be processed.

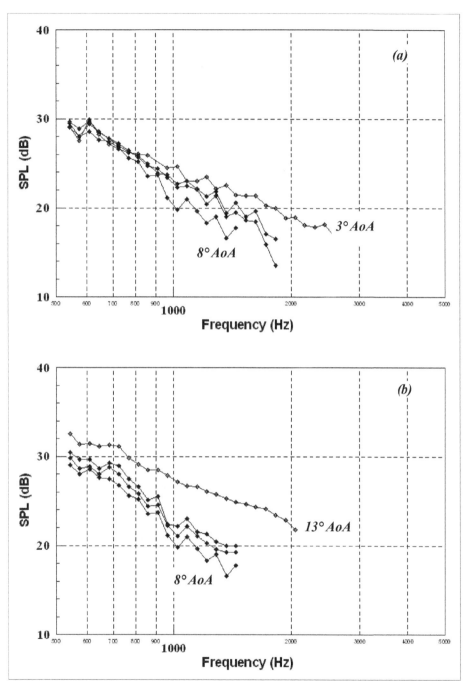

Figure 189. Integrated spectrum for untripped B1-18 airfoil at (a) 3°, 6°, 7°, and 8° and (b) 8°, 10°, 11°, and 13° effective AoA for 28 m/s (nominal chord Reynolds number: 1,500,000) (scale one-twelfth octave bands; tunnel entry: July 2007)

206

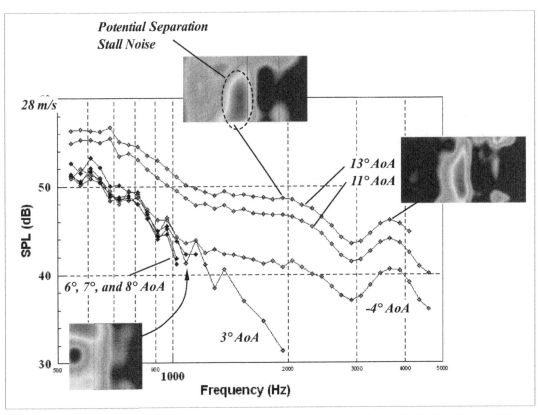

Figure 190. Integrated spectrum for untripped B1-18 airfoil at -4°, 3°, 6°, 7°, 8°, 11°, and 13° effective AoA for 54 m/s (nominal chord Reynolds number: 3,200,000) (scale one-twelfth octave bands. Tunnel entry: July (black) and Nov.-Dec. (blue) 2007)

As listed in Table 11, measurements with the boundary layer tripped were performed for only the -3° and 6° angles of attack. The data file for the 7° angle of attack was corrupted and the data could not be processed. Figure 191(a) and (b) show the results for the tripped boundary-layer cases (shown in red). The corresponding no-trip results (shown in black) also are plotted. It is clear that tripping the boundary layer has a minor effect—for example an approximate reduction of 1 dB to 2 dB at 28 m/s for frequencies above 1,000 Hz. The result for soiled configuration is undistinguishable from the tripped case. The scaled spectra are shown in Figures 211 and 212. As was the case for the other airfoils, the data scale well with the fifth power except for the stalled conditions.

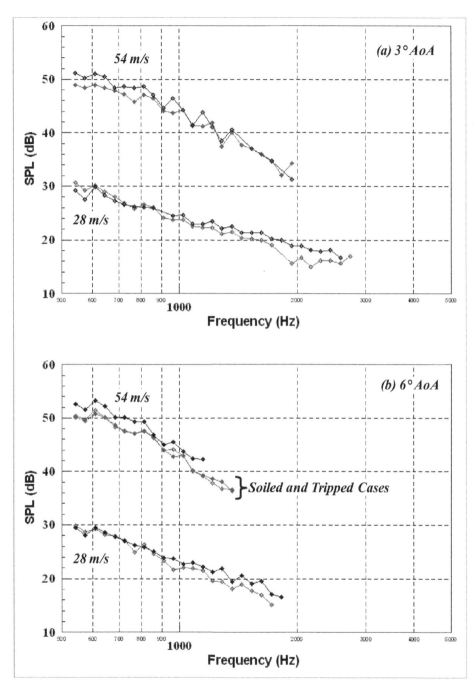

Figure 191. Integrated spectrum for untripped (black) and tripped (red) Risø airfoil at (a) 3° and (b) 3° effective AoA for 28 m/s and 54 m/s (nominal chord Reynolds number 1,500,000–3,200,000) (scale: one-twelfth octave bands; tunnel entry: July 2007)

4.5.5. S831 Airfoil

The test matrix for the S831 airfoil is shown in Table 14. Most of the test configurations again were measured during the July tunnel entry. Measurements were performed for two flow speeds (28 m/s, 54 m/s), effective angle of attack from -7° to 8°, and both untripped and tripped boundary-layer conditions. Figure 192 shows the noise spectrum for all the untripped cases for both speeds (including only data at the frequency bands where trailing-edge noise was identified in the acoustic maps). Unlike the previous DU96 and Risø airfoils, the S831 model shows significant scattering as a function of the angle of attack, in particular above 800 Hz. The 8° angle of attack for the higher flow-speed case doesn't follow this trend, however, and instead shows a significant jump (~6 dB) for the whole spectrum. Similar to the Risø B1-18 airfoil, this increase in the spectrum could be due to flow-separation effects. To help better identify trends, the results again are plotted in Figure 193(a) and (b) for the 28 m/s and 54 m/s flow speed separately, and only for the July entry. These figures show opposite behavior for the two flow speeds. For the greater speed the levels increase with the angle of attack. At the lower flow speed the noise levels are reduced as the angle of attack increases from the no lift (-7°) case to angles greater than 3°. Beyond this angle the noise seems insensitive to the angle of attack.

Table 14. Test Matrix for Microphone Phased Array Measurements of S831 Airfoil

Airfoil	Effective AoA (deg)	Trip	Flow Speed (m/s)	Fan Speed (rpm)	Tunnel Temp. (°F)	Run Number	Date
S831	-7	No trip	29	277	80.1	82	7/11/2007
S831	-7	No trip	60	567	83.4	83	7/11/2007
S831	-2	No trip	29	286	76.1	84	7/11/2007
S831	-2	No trip	56	557	70.7	146	7/25/2007
S831	0	No trip	56	569	70.0	147	7/25/2007
S831	3	No trip	29	315	83.2	85	7/11/2007
S831	3	No trip	56	584	71.5	148	7/25/2007
S831	5	No trip	30	324	87.5	86	7/11/2007
S831	5	No trip	57	593	70.2	149	7/25/2007
S831	5	No trip	28	254	38.9	54	12/3/2007
S831	5	No trip	53	506	43.5	55	12/3/2007
S831	6	No trip	56	595	71.3	150	7/25/2007
S831	6	No trip	30	329	86.5	87	7/11/2007
S831	7	No trip	30	328	85.3	88	7/11/2007
S831	7	No trip	56	605	71.7	151[1]	7/25/2007
S831	8	No trip	29	315	80.0	89	7/11/2007
S831	8	No trip	57	633	73.7	152	7/25/2007
S831	8	No trip	53	509	45.3	56	12/3/2007
S831	-2	Tripped	30	310	95.0	90	7/12/2007
S831	-2	Tripped	56	551	69.9	145	7/25/2007
S831	5	Tripped	56	595	69.9	144	7/25/2007
S831	5	Tripped	30	311	95.3	91	7/12/2007
S831	5	Soiled	57	586	71.6	153	7/26/2007

Notes
1. Data file was corrupted and case could not be processed.

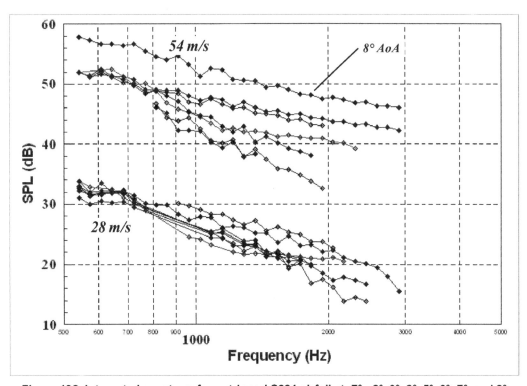

Figure 192. Integrated spectrum for untripped S831 airfoil at -7°, -2°, 0°, 3°, 5°, 6°, 7°, and 8° effective AoA for 28 m/s and 54 m/s (nominal chord Reynolds number 1,500,000–3,200,000) (scale: one-twelfth octave bands; tunnel entry: July (black), November-December (blue) 2007)

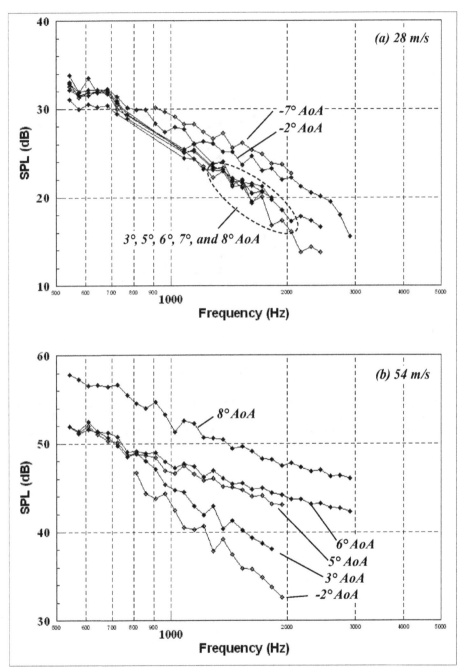

Figure 193. Integrated spectrum for untripped S831 airfoil as a function of AoA at (a) 28 m/s and (b) 54 m/s (nominal chord Reynolds number 1,500,000–3,200,000) (scale: one-twelfth octave bands; tunnel entry: July 2007)

211

The reason for the unusual behavior described above is not clear. The S831 airfoil, however, shows some flow anomalies that were measured by the array (as well as the aerodynamic data). Figure 194(a) shows the acoustic maps for the S831 airfoil at -7° angle of attack at 28 m/s for two one-twelfth octave frequency bands (816 Hz, 1,024 Hz). These acoustic images reveal a strong noise source close to the leading edge of the airfoil, strongly suggesting a flow anomaly (e.g., separation bubbles). This leading-edge noise source is observed clearly in all frequency bands that are 816 Hz and higher. To gain insight, a two-dimensional computational fluid dynamics (CFD) calculation of the flow field around the airfoil for the -7° angle of attack at 28 m/s case was performed using a k-ε turbulent model. Figure 194(b) shows the streamlines around the airfoil and a zoomed-in view on the leading edge. The presence of a separation bubble is confirmed by the CFD predictions. The pressure data (Section 3.1 above) also confirmed a potential flow separation. Similar acoustic results also were observed in the case of the higher Reynolds number (54 m/s) at the same -7° angle of attack. Although not as clear, similar leading-edge noise around 812 Hz also can be observed in the case of the higher Reynolds number (54 m/s) at 5° angle of attack for both the clean and soiled conditions, but it completely vanishes when tripped. This effect can be observed in the acoustic maps for these three cases (Figure 195).

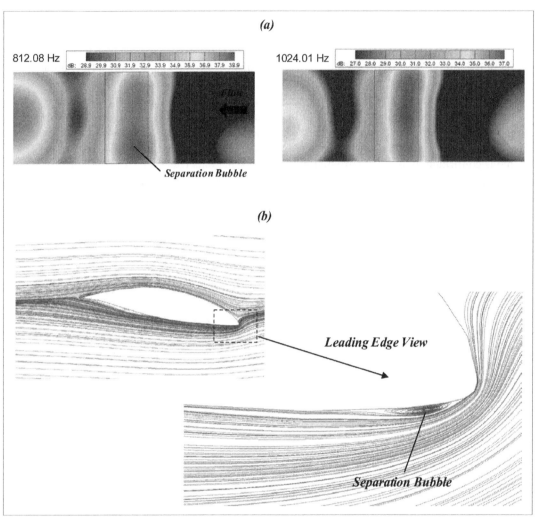

Figure 194. Acoustic maps for (a) S831 airfoil at -7° effective AoA at 28 m/s (Re = 1,500,000) and (b) two-dimensional CFD solution showing a separation bubble near the leading edge on the pressure side

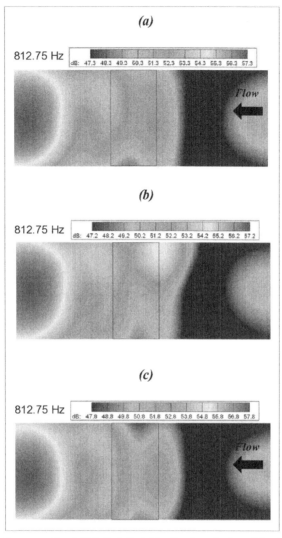

Figure 195. Acoustic maps for S831 airfoil at 5° effective AoA at 54 m/s (Re = 3,200,000): (a) no trip, (b) tripped, (c) soiled

As listed in Table 14, measurements with the boundary layer tripped were performed for only the -2° and 5° angles of attack. Figure 196(a) and (b) show the results for the tripped boundary-layer cases (red) as well as the no-trip results (black). It is clear that tripping the boundary layer has a minor effect (e.g., an approximate reduction of 1dB to 2 dB at 28 m/s for frequencies greater than 1,000 Hz). The result for soiled configuration again is indistinguishable from that of the tripped case. The normalized spectra are shown in Figures 213 and 214. For this particular airfoil, the data didn't scale well with the fifth power law.

214

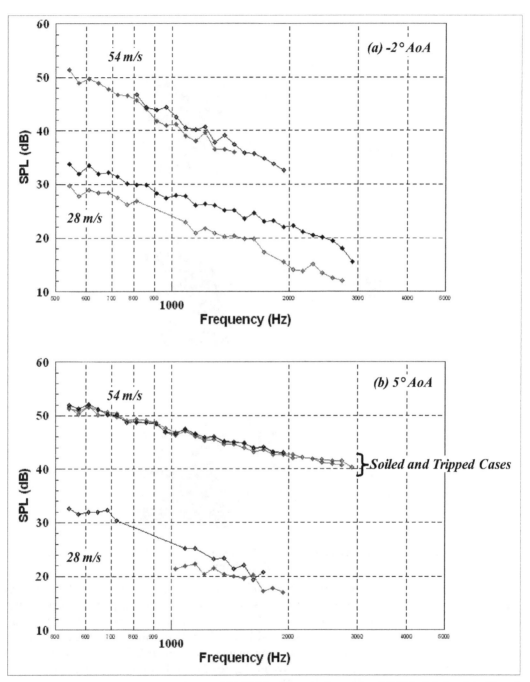

Figure 196. Integrated spectrum for untripped (black) and tripped (red) S831 airfoil at (a) -2° and (b) 5° effective AoA for 28 m/s and 54 m/s (nominal chord Reynolds number 1,500,000–3,200,000) (scale: one-twelfth octave bands; tunnel entry: July 2007)

4.5.6. Airfoil Trailing-Edge Noise Comparison

This section presents a direct comparison of the trailing-edge noise from the 4 airfoils tested at Reynolds numbers of 1,500,000 and 3,200,000. The NACA 0012 airfoil is the only model that showed vortex shedding at angles of attack greater than 6°, therefore only data for 0°, 2°, 4°, and 6° are included. Figure 197 shows the untripped trailing-edge noise spectra for the 4 airfoils. For clarity, the stalled conditions in these plots are indicated. The tripped conditions are shown in Figure 198 together with the corresponding no-trip cases. All the tripped cases were measured at small angles of attack for all 4 airfoils, therefore the no-trip cases for angles of attack greater than 6° were deleted from these plots, i.e. no stalled cases. Inspection of Figure 197 and Figure 198 shows a clearly striking overall difference in the acoustic behavior between models. The most important differences are summarized below.

- At both Reynolds numbers, the noise spectrum for the NACA 0012 airfoil clearly is different from that of the three wind-turbine airfoils in both levels and shape.

- Tripping the boundary layer leads to noise reduction only for the NACA 0012 and DU96 airfoils at the lower Reynolds number.

- The S831 airfoil noise shows the greatest dependence upon angle of attack at the higher Reynolds number. The other models appear to be less sensitive to angle of attack than the S831.

- Separation-stall noise is characterized by an increase of at least 8-10 dB across the whole spectrum relative to pre-stall conditions.

- Particularly for small angles of attack without the presence of vortex shedding, the noise-level scales well with the fifth power of the free-stream velocity for the NACA 0012, DU96, and B1-18. The S831 airfoil data didn't collapse with the 5th power law. The scaling analysis is discussed in greater detail in Appendix C.

216

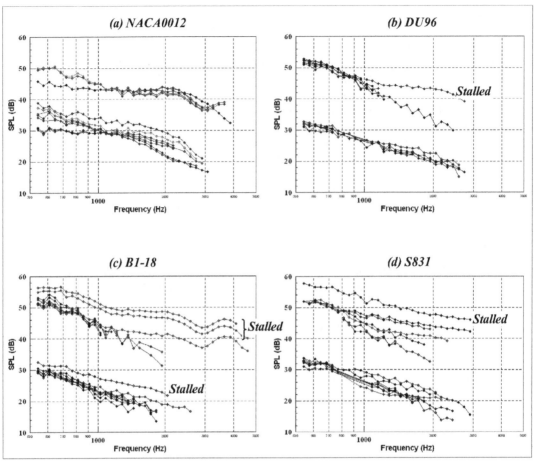

Figure 197. Integrated spectrum for untripped (a) NACA0012, (b) DU96, (c) Risø, and (d) S831 airfoils at Reynolds numbers of 1,500,000 and 3,200,000

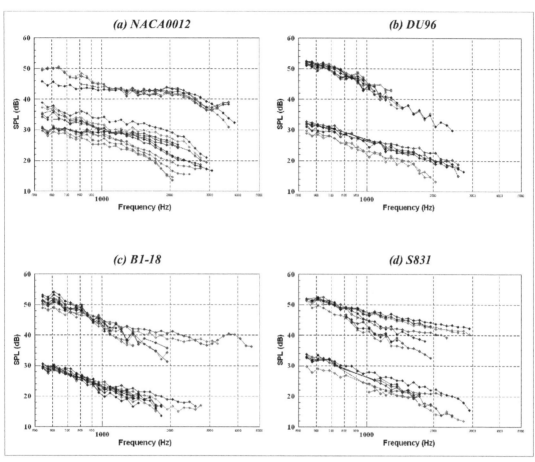

Figure 198. Integrated spectrum for untripped and tripped (a) NACA 0012, (b) DU96, (c) Risø, and (d) S831 airfoils at Reynolds number of 1,500,000 and 3,200,000

5. Summary

Aerodynamic and acoustic measurements of three wind turbine airfoils with a 0.914-m chord were tested at the Virginia Polytechnic Institute and State University Stability Wind Tunnel, in its anechoic configuration. The models used were the Delft DU96, Risø B1-18, and NREL S831. A NACA 0012 model of the same chord also was tested. The four models were tested for a range of flow conditions, with nominal chord Reynolds numbers of from 800,000 to 3,800,000. The Virginia Tech Stability Tunnel aeroacoustic configuration is new, therefore noise measurements of a small 0.2-m chord NACA 0012 airfoil also were obtained (referred to as small NACA). Results for this small-size airfoil were compared to data obtained in an open-jet aeroacoustic tunnel with a NACA 0012 model of almost the same chord (Brooks et al. 1989). Results obtained using the Virginia Tech wind tunnel are in good agreement with those obtained by Brooks et al. (1989). This comparison provided the first validation of the capabilities of the new Virginia Tech anechoic tunnel.

The aerodynamic flow measurements of the NACA 0012, DU96, B1-18, and S831 airfoils consisted of static-pressure distributions on the airfoil surfaces, wake-profile measurements downstream of the mid-span of the airfoil, and single hot-wire measurements in the vicinity of the trailing edge. The hot-wire measurements were performed for DU96, B1-18, and S831 airfoils. The noise measurements consisted of far-field acoustic data using 63-microphone phased array systems of all models.

The mean-pressure distributions were used in conjunction with a panel-method code (for free-flight conditions) to compute effective angles of attack. Interestingly, the interference correction was found to be 22% for all cases (i.e. independent of the airfoil profile). Pressure distributions also were used to compute lift and pitching moment. Wake measurements were performed and used to estimate drag. A single hot-wire probe also was used to measure trailing-edge boundary layers near the trailing edge for the DU96, B1-18, and S831 airfoils.

Noise measurements using the phased arrays were successful in identifying trailing-edge noise for most of the configurations, in particular for the lower angles of attack. At greater angles, junction vortices at the leading edge of the airfoils and the resulting turbulence interacting with the trailing edge produced sources that masked the trailing-edge noise. This effect appeared in both tunnel entries, although it was less significant in the second entry after the test modifications were implemented. Thus, when interpreting the results and drawing conclusions, it is important to remember that self-noise data at the greater angles of attack are limited.

The measurements revealed significant differences and similarities in the noise characteristic of the wind-turbine airfoils. The first and likely most important similarity is that the DU96, B1-18, and S831 airfoils did not show any vortex shedding. Conversely, the NACA 0012 did shed vortices from the trailing edge at an angle of attack greater than 6°. Tripping the boundary layer was only marginally effective in alleviating this problem. The vortex shedding from the NACA 0012 at high Reynolds numbers has been observed in previous experiments (Paterson et al. 1973).

Differences in the noise characteristics are more numerous. The DU96 airfoil trailing-edge noise seems to be rather insensitive to the angle of attack, in particular at the lower flow speed of 28 m/s (Re = 1,500,000). The B1-18 and S831, however, clearly show an increase in noise with increasing angle of attack—which was more dramatic at the highest Reynolds number measured (3,200,000). A flow anomaly (separation bubble) for the S831 model at the zero lift (-7°) configuration also was found. The flow irregularity was identified by the mean-pressure measurement, and was supported by two-dimensional CFD predictions. From the noise maps, it appears that this flow irregularity near the leading edge still persisted even at greater angles of attack (5°). Another important difference is that tripping the boundary layer leads to noise reduction only for the DU96 airfoil at the lower flow speed of 28 m/s. Acoustically, there is no convincing effect of tripping the boundary layer for any of the airfoils at the greatest speed tested (Re = 3,200,000). The trip using random distribution of silicon carbide grit particles on the leading-edge region (soiled trip) did not result in any noticeable noise increase. The acoustic data scaled well with the fifth power of the free-stream velocity.

Despite the difficulties and limitations found during these experiments, they yielded a set of useful flow and noise results enabling formation of an initial experimental database of aerodynamic and aeroacoustic measurements for wind-turbine airfoils at high Reynolds numbers. It is possible to improve the noise results by reprocessing the data using more advanced (but time consuming) beamforming algorithms.

6. References

Bearman, P. W. (1971). "Corrections for the Effect of Ambient Temperature Drift on Hot-Wire Measurements in Incompressible Flow." *DISA Information*, 11, pp. 25–30.

Brooks, T. F.; Pope, D. S.; Marcolini, M. A. (1989). *Airfoil Self Noise and Prediction.* NASA-RP-1218.

Choi, K.; Simpson, R. L. (1987). *Some Mean Velocity, Turbulence and Unsteadiness Characteristics of the VPI & SU Stability Wind Tunnel.* Report VPI-Aero-161. Blacksburg, VA: Department of Aerospace and Ocean Engineering, Virginia Polytechnic Institute and State University.

Crede, E. (2008). *Aerodynamics and Acoustics of the Virginia Tech Stability Tunnel Anechoic System.* Master's Thesis. Blacksburg, VA: Virginia Polytechnic Institute and State University. Available at http://scholar.lib.vt.edu/theses/available/etd-08112008-094223/unrestricted/ Thesis.pdf. Accessed September 5, 2009.

Devenport, W.; Burdisso, R. A. (April 2008). "Aeroacoustic Testing of Sandia National Labs Wind Turbine Airfoils." *Virginia Tech Report.*

Jaeger, S. M.; Horne, W. C.; Allen, C. S. (2000). "Effect of Surface Treatment on Array Microphone Self-Noise." Prepared for the 6th AIAA/CEAS Aeroacoustics Conference, June 2000. AIAA Paper 2000-1937. Mountainview, CA: Aerospace Computing, Inc. 10 pp.

Kuethe, A.; Chow, C. (1986). *Foundations of Aerodynamics: Bases of Aerodynamic Design,* 4th Edition, New York: John Wiley & Sons.

Paterson, R.W.; Vogt, P.G.; Fink M.R. (1973) "Vortex Noise of Isolated Airfoils," *J. Aircraft*, Vol. 10, No. 5, Mau.

Remillieux, M. C.; Camargo, H. E.; Burdisso, R. A. (2007). "Calibration of a Microphone Phased-Array for Amplitude in the Virginia Tech Anechoic Wind Tunnel." Prepared for NOISE-CON 2007, October 2007.

Remillieux, M. C.; Camargo, H. E.; Burdisso, R. A.; Ng Wing, F. (2007). "Aeroacoustic Study of a 26%-Scale, High-Fidelity, Boeing 777 Main Landing Gear in a Semi-Anechoic Wind-Tunnel Test Section." Prepared for Proceedings of the 13th AIAA/CEAS Aeroacoustics Conference (28th AIAA Aeroacoustics Conference), May 2007. AIAA-2007-3453.

Remillieux, M.; Crede, E.; Camargo, H.; Burdisso, R.; Devenport, W.; Rasnick, M.; van Seeters, P.; Chou, A. (2008). "Calibration and Demonstration of the New Virginia Tech Anechoic Wind Tunnel." *Proceedings of the 14th AIAA/CEAS Aeroacoustics Meeting*, May 2008. AIAA-2008-2911.

Staubs, J. (May 2008). *Real Airfoil Effects on Leading Edge Noise*. Ph.D. Dissertation. Blacksburg, VA: Virginia Polytechnic Institute and State University. Available at http://scholar.lib.vt.edu/theses/available/etd-05282008-002246/unrestricted/ JKS_Dissertation.pdf. Accessed September 5, 2009.

Appendix A. Wing Section Measurements

The four airfoil models used in this study were measured to determine the deviations from the design profiles. For each model (NACA 0012, B1-18, DU96, S831), the section shape was measured at four locations along the span (¼ span, midspan, ¾ span, and at the pressure taps access hatch). Measurements were made with a FaroArm CMM (model Fusion) connected to a laptop PC running a Windows version of CAM2 Measure X (CMM control software). The FaroArm (Figure 199) was used with a 3-mm diameter spherical probe and provides 0.1-mm measurement accuracy.

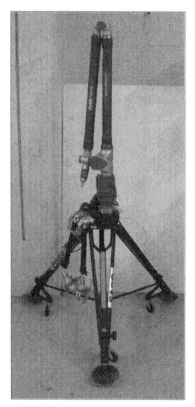

Figure 199. FARO Fusion Arm CMM used for measuring the manufactured wing models

The resulting measurements are presented in Figures 200 through 203 for the NACA 0012, B1-18, DU96, and S831, respectively. Each figure is composed of three different plots.

- The top plot presents a direct comparison between the measured and design profiles, plotted in terms of their chord-aligned airfoil coordinates (*x* and *y*, as described in Section 3) normalized on the airfoil chord.

- The difference between the measured and design profiles (defined as the distance between the two profiles along the direction normal to the measured section and expressed as percentage of the chord) is plotted in the middle chart against the normalized edge-length *s/c* (defined in Section 3.1). A positive difference implies that the measured profile is thicker than the design shape.

- The measured and design profiles are used as an input in a linear-vortex panel method code to determine the influence of the section shape deviations on the pressure distribution. The resulting pressure distributions are shown in the bottom plot for an effective angle of attack of 8°.

For each figure the sections measured at the ¼ span, midspan, ¾ span, and at the pressure taps access hatch are plotted as blue, green, magenta, and red curves, and the associated design profile is shown in black.

For the NACA 0012 model, examination of Figure 200(b) shows that at ¼ span, midspan, and ¾ span the shape has an offset on the order of 0.1% chord (0.9 mm) on most of the suction side of the wing (positive *y/c* or *s/c* of less than 1). On the pressure side (negative *y/c* or *s/c* greater than 1), the offset from the design increases from 0.1% chord at the leading edge to about 0.25% chord (2.3 mm) at the trailing edge. The consistently positive offset at ¼ span, midspan, and ¾ span suggests that the model was manufactured 1 mm to 2.3 mm too thick as compared to the design shape. The same type of deviation behaviors can be observed at the pressure ports hatch location. The offset is relatively constant on the suction side (and less than 0.5 mm) although it consistently increases on the pressure side, from 0.23% chord (2.1 mm) at the leading edge to 0.37% chord (3.4 mm) at the trailing edge. Such positive offset on the pressure side suggests that the hatch is raised above the rest of the wing surface by 1 mm to 1.5 mm. These differences in profile shape do not seem to lead to significant changes in the pressure distribution other than near the location of minimum pressure as seen in Figure 200(c). Due to the increased thickness, the magnitude of the minimum pressure is increased at the ¼ span, midspan, and ¾ span. At the hatch, the pressure distribution is remarkably close to the design loading (a result in agreement with the measured pressure distribution at 8° presented in Figure 30).

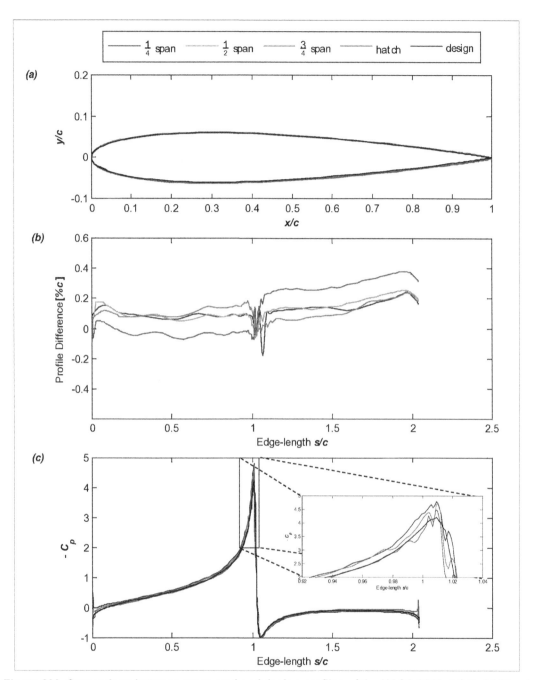

Figure 200. Comparison between measured and design profiles of the NACA 0012 airfoil; (a) Direct comparison between measured and design profiles, (b) profile difference (defined as the distance between measured and design profiles along the direction normal to the measured section), (c) vortex panel method pressure distributions obtained from the measured and design profiles at an effective angle of attack of 8°

224

The measured profiles around the B1-18 model and the associated pressure distributions are presented in Figure 201. The B1-18 profile is proprietary, therefore Figure 201(a) intentionally is left blank. Figure 201(b) shows that most of the profile differences are greater on the suction side ($s/c < 1$) than on the pressure side ($s/c > 1$). This is also apparent by looking at Figure 201(c) in which the pressure distribution on the pressure side shows little deviation from the design loading. On the suction side, Figure 201(b) shows that the model was manufactured with a greater thickness than the design shape. As expected, the increased thickness results in a lower pressure on the suction side as compared to the design shape (clearly seen in the leading-edge area blow-up of Figure 201(c)). Figure 53 shows that the panel method predicts a pressure in the leading-edge area on the suction side that is lower than that which actually was measured. It should be noted, however, that the model was assumed to have the design shape when the lift interference corrections were computed. It therefore is possible that the difference in the airfoil shape could result in a different correction.

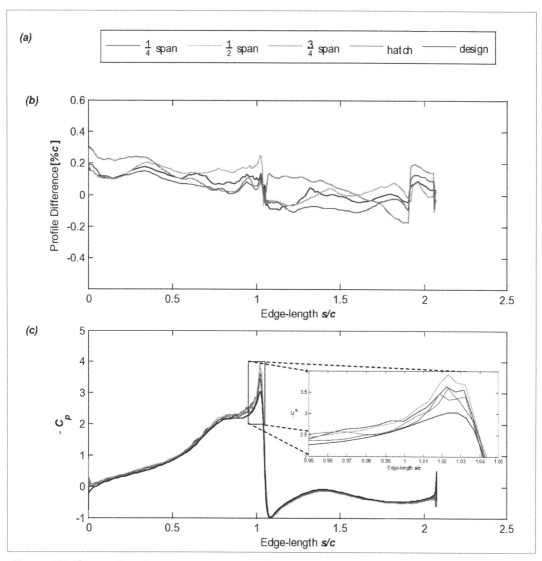

Figure 201. Comparison between measured and design profiles of the B1-18 airfoil; (a) the direct comparison between measured and design profiles is intentionally not included (see text), (b) profile difference (defined as the distance between measured and design profiles along the direction normal to the measured section), (c) vortex panel method pressure distributions obtained from the measured and design profiles at an effective angle of attack of 8°

The measurements on the DU96 are provided in Figure 202. Visual inspection of Figure 202(a) shows that the manufactured wing has a consistently smaller thickness than the design shape. This observation is confirmed by Figure 202(b) that shows maximum negative deviations of up to 0.6% chord (5.5 mm) from the design profile. Not only are these deviations quite great, but the region where they occur is particularly important. Independently of the spanwise location, the deviation from the design shape reaches two minima around $s/c = 0.7$ and 1.37. These locations correspond to 30% chord on the suction side and 35% chord on the pressure side, respectively, which coincides with the location of maximum thickness. It therefore is not surprising to observe that these changes in the maximum thickness result in significant variations in the associated pressure distributions (Figure 202(c)). This plot is important because it shows that the difference between the pressure distributions associated with the measured profile at the hatch (red curve) and design profile (a difference of 0.1 to 0.2 (in terms of C_p) on the suction side) is very similar to the difference between the measured pressure distribution and the design pressure distribution (0.1 to 0.15 (in terms of C_p) on the suction side, as shown in Figure 70). It therefore follows that the difference observed between the measured pressure distribution and design distribution could be due mostly to the uncertainty in the model fabrication. Also note that the DU96 is the model that displays the greatest deviations from the design shape (up to 0.6% chord or 5.5 mm).

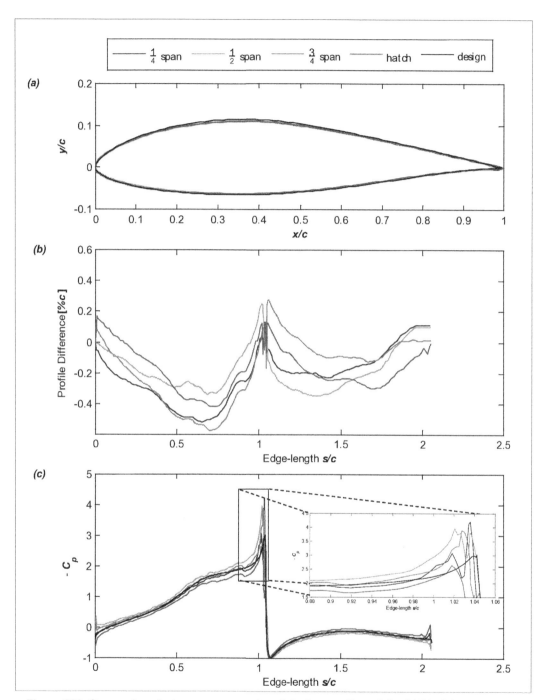

Figure 202. Comparison between measured and design profiles of the DU96 airfoil; (a) direct comparison between measured and design profiles, (b) profile difference (defined as the distance between measured and design profiles along the direction normal to the measured section), (c) vortex panel method pressure distributions obtained from the measured and design profiles at an effective angle of attack of 8°

The S831 measurements are presented in Figure 203. Figure 203(b) shows that the manufactured model is sizably thicker than the design shape except for the first 50% chord on the suction side of the wing ($0.5 < s/c < 1$). The profile differences are particularly noticeable near the leading edge on the pressure side ($1.05 < s/c < 1.2$) where the maximum deviation of 0.25% chord (2.3 mm) occurs. Such deviation also occurs near the trailing edge on the suction side ($s/c \approx 0$). These variations in the model shape result in deviation from the design pressure distribution as shown in Figure 203(c). Interestingly, the pressure distribution obtained from the profile measured at the hatch shows good agreement with the design loading, even to the point of minimum pressure. Figure 92 shows that the measured pressure distribution, however, was significantly lower than the design loading. As mentioned earlier, the discrepancy could be the result of an error in the lift-interference correction originating from the use of the incorrect surface geometry. Additionally, the spanwise variation in the wing loading shown in Figure 203(c) could have resulted in three-dimensional effects on the model surface, and therefore might have contaminated the measured pressure distribution.

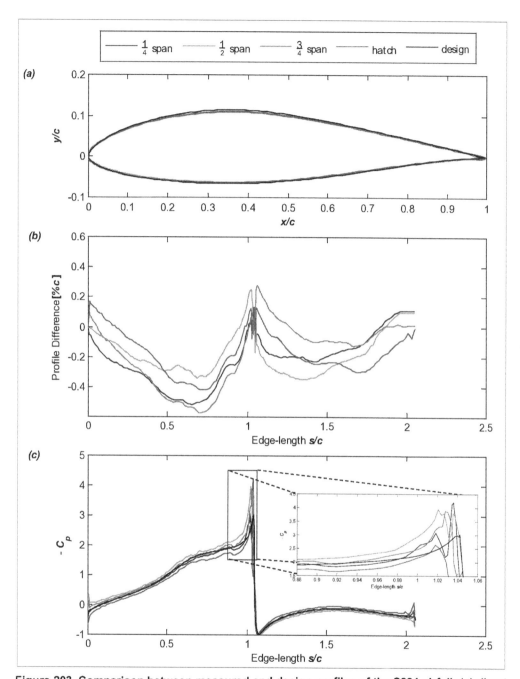

Figure 203. Comparison between measured and design profiles of the S831 airfoil; (a) direct comparison between measured and design profiles, (b) profile difference (defined as the distance between measured and design profiles along the direction normal to the measured section), (c) vortex panel method pressure distributions obtained from the measured and design profiles at an effective angle of attack of 8°

Finally, the CMM also was used to measure the location of the pressure ports on the manufactured models. The measured coordinates are presented for the NACA 0012, DU96, and S831 in Table 15 through Table 17.

Table 15. Measured Pressure Taps Location for the NACA 0012 Model

Tap #	Suction Side			Pressure Side		
	x/c	y/c	z/c	x/c	y/c	z/c
1	9.84E-05	0.00155	-0.93107	0.002824	-0.00907	-1.05983
2	0.003155	0.010315	-0.93457	0.004078	-0.01081	-1.05745
3	0.006373	0.014396	-0.93336	0.008392	-0.01598	-1.05609
4	0.008506	0.016504	-0.93556	0.01092	-0.01778	-1.05572
5	0.00989	0.017523	-0.93485	0.013053	-0.01921	-1.05347
6	0.012893	0.019943	-0.93721	0.014167	-0.02003	-1.05487
7	0.015599	0.02206	-0.93742	0.016989	-0.02218	-1.05422
8	0.017301	0.02307	-0.9361	0.018561	-0.02324	-1.05389
9	0.018616	0.02385	-0.93716	0.026836	-0.02706	-1.05268
10	0.025311	0.027385	-0.93942	0.051504	-0.03661	-1.0467
11	0.051362	0.037278	-0.94345	0.074813	-0.0427	-1.04242
12	0.074043	0.042995	-0.95007	0.099902	-0.04748	-1.0351
13	0.102196	0.048369	-0.95588	0.125015	-0.05135	-1.02953
14	0.12745	0.052024	-0.9613	0.148143	-0.05411	-1.02343
15	0.152295	0.054726	-0.96659	0.173138	-0.05639	-1.01796
16	0.175494	0.056795	-0.97443	0.201575	-0.05829	-1.01177
17	0.200654	0.058465	-0.97851	0.225214	-0.05952	-1.00806
18	0.2274	0.059804	-0.98424	0.250292	-0.06037	-1.00064
19	0.277839	0.061173	-0.99593	0.273898	-0.06074	-0.99471
20	0.300704	0.061251	-1.00329	0.300221	-0.06089	-0.99059
21	0.325758	0.061127	-1.00756	0.325485	-0.06067	-0.98483
22	0.350956	0.060607	-1.01306	0.348741	-0.06047	-0.97726
23	0.377668	0.059893	-1.0194	0.375192	-0.05991	-0.97331
24	0.400979	0.059047	-1.0267	0.400331	-0.05915	-0.96418
25	0.425695	0.058016	-1.03097	0.426458	-0.05811	-0.96057
26	0.451503	0.05661	-1.03713	0.450156	-0.05703	-0.95417
27	0.47749	0.055332	-1.04118	0.475357	-0.05568	-0.94837
28	0.49918	0.054048	-1.04687	0.500399	-0.05428	-0.94443
29	0.550643	0.050713	-1.05616	0.549989	-0.051	-0.93014
30	0.601116	0.047012	-1.04502	0.600667	-0.04718	-0.94299
31	0.652969	0.042463	-1.03487	0.650945	-0.04294	-0.95585
32	0.702829	0.037561	-1.02372	0.700593	-0.03833	-0.96462
33	0.750993	0.032556	-1.01323	0.750228	-0.03336	-0.97804
34	0.801141	0.02714	-1.00215	0.799282	-0.02808	-0.98947
35	0.851095	0.021529	-0.9887	0.850503	-0.02216	-0.99916

	Suction Side			Pressure Side		
Tap #	x/c	y/c	z/c	x/c	y/c	z/c
36	0.901626	0.015557	-0.9772	0.900398	-0.016	-1.01265
37	0.921456	0.013087	-0.97252	0.920683	-0.01329	-1.01558
38	0.939591	0.010697	-0.96806	0.938922	-0.01077	-1.02178
39	0.960936	0.007788	-0.96314	0.960496	-0.00763	-1.02629
40	0.982035	0.004224	-0.95857	0.980536	-0.00461	-1.02934

Table 16. Measured Pressure Taps Location for the DU96 Model

	Suction Side			Pressure Side		
Tap #	x/c	y/c	z/c	x/c	y/c	z/c
1	0.003292	0.011995	-1.3942	0.000854	-0.00565	-1.26718
2	0.006171	0.015623	-1.38964	0.000911	-0.00577	-1.22113
3	0.00922	0.018909	-1.39099	0.001678	-0.0073	-1.22098
4	0.010154	0.019839	-1.39042	0.002752	-0.00863	-1.22084
5	0.013419	0.022889	-1.392	0.002796	-0.00857	-1.26764
6	0.016083	0.025185	-1.39054	0.004044	-0.0099	-1.22068
7	0.017281	0.02617	-1.38893	0.00544	-0.01119	-1.27064
8	0.02206	0.029853	-1.38773	0.007695	-0.01299	-1.26927
9	0.048202	0.045765	-1.38361	0.01033	-0.01486	-1.26951
10	0.074082	0.05795	-1.37583	0.013293	-0.01677	-1.27079
11	0.100009	0.068147	-1.37045	0.015552	-0.01811	-1.26927
12	0.12343	0.076129	-1.36237	0.018681	-0.01983	-1.26992
13	0.149184	0.083665	-1.35856	0.07332	-0.03849	-1.28323
14	0.174394	0.08991	-1.35277	0.096759	-0.04359	-1.29056
15	0.197125	0.094688	-1.34697	0.125797	-0.04859	-1.29678
16	0.223405	0.099349	-1.33941	0.149663	-0.05193	-1.30109
17	0.248699	0.103042	-1.33523	0.173986	-0.05474	-1.30844
18	0.27201	0.105778	-1.32985	0.198674	-0.05704	-1.31364
19	0.296888	0.107984	-1.32393	0.222899	-0.05879	-1.31985
20	0.322516	0.109478	-1.31889	0.246907	-0.06021	-1.32519
21	0.348243	0.110215	-1.31491	0.273438	-0.0614	-1.33115
22	0.373451	0.11023	-1.30569	0.299987	-0.06216	-1.33697
23	0.398311	0.109564	-1.30133	0.323587	-0.06254	-1.3427
24	0.422993	0.108208	-1.29514	0.350657	-0.06261	-1.34841
25	0.447856	0.106142	-1.29136	0.372243	-0.06239	-1.35316
26	0.474186	0.103351	-1.28393	0.398174	-0.06184	-1.36015
27	0.498357	0.100354	-1.27672	0.424065	-0.06093	-1.36588
28	0.549352	0.092895	-1.26626	0.446895	-0.05981	-1.37243
29	0.597992	0.084761	-1.27802	0.471678	-0.05826	-1.37726
30	0.648524	0.075557	-1.28986	0.499128	-0.05614	-1.3829

232

Tap #	Suction Side x/c	Suction Side y/c	Suction Side z/c	Pressure Side x/c	Pressure Side y/c	Pressure Side z/c
31	0.696585	0.066204	-1.30128	0.546927	-0.05147	-1.39402
32	0.747025	0.056086	-1.31315	0.598768	-0.04527	-1.38139
33	0.798813	0.045484	-1.32663	0.646769	-0.0388	-1.37208
34	0.848341	0.035031	-1.33653	0.697434	-0.0315	-1.36065
35	0.899085	0.024063	-1.34649	0.710651	-0.02959	-1.22352
36	0.918749	0.019844	-1.3528	0.711728	-0.02944	-1.22237
37	0.938233	0.015491	-1.3572	0.712803	-0.02928	-1.22122
38	0.959148	0.01093	-1.36243	0.713879	-0.02913	-1.22006
39	0.979041	0.006548	-1.36695	0.748834	-0.02406	-1.34861
40				0.799684	-0.01689	-1.33766
41				0.848019	-0.01068	-1.32439
42				0.89811	-0.0051	-1.31206
43				0.918486	-0.00332	-1.30975
44				0.938007	-0.00202	-1.3054
45				0.957932	-0.00027	-1.29924
46				0.977996	-4.3E-05	-1.29593

Table 17. Measured Pressure Taps Location for the S-831 Model

Tap #	Suction Side x/c	Suction Side y/c	Suction Side z/c	Pressure Side x/c	Pressure Side y/c	Pressure Side z/c
1	0.00313	0.00841	-1.47328	0.00055	-0.00318	-1.34733
2	0.00589	0.01234	-1.47299	0.00388	-0.00724	-1.34927
3	0.00858	0.01592	-1.47213	0.00582	-0.00914	-1.34977
4	0.01028	0.01787	-1.47328	0.00837	-0.01018	-1.34738
5	0.01362	0.02121	-1.47143	0.01101	-0.01105	-1.35111
6	0.01561	0.02326	-1.47209	0.01334	-0.01174	-1.35009
7	0.01706	0.02469	-1.47013	0.01630	-0.01247	-1.35237
8	0.01949	0.02674	-1.46959	0.01825	-0.01282	-1.35165
9	0.02516	0.03153	-1.47007	0.02128	-0.01329	-1.35226
10	0.05025	0.04789	-1.46121	0.02605	-0.01412	-1.35500
11	0.07379	0.05987	-1.45705	0.05121	-0.01787	-1.35722
12	0.09890	0.07078	-1.45111	0.07392	-0.02043	-1.36426
13	0.12538	0.08072	-1.44708	0.09992	-0.02313	-1.37063
14	0.15050	0.08919	-1.44123	0.12594	-0.02574	-1.37799
15	0.17713	0.09712	-1.43395	0.15022	-0.02794	-1.38182
16	0.19925	0.10306	-1.42797	0.17479	-0.03006	-1.38739
17	0.22723	0.10995	-1.42238	0.20122	-0.03212	-1.39369
18	0.25036	0.11482	-1.41663	0.22552	-0.03389	-1.40152
19	0.27558	0.11992	-1.41247	0.25038	-0.03551	-1.40634

233

Tap #	Suction Side			Pressure Side		
	x/c	y/c	z/c	x/c	y/c	z/c
20	0.30444	0.12450	-1.40481	0.27641	-0.03709	-1.40959
21	0.32390	0.12772	-1.39922	0.29937	-0.03838	-1.41476
22	0.35063	0.13092	-1.39183	0.32478	-0.03964	-1.42306
23	0.37569	0.13362	-1.38610	0.35085	-0.04071	-1.42886
24	0.40081	0.13604	-1.38182	0.37568	-0.04145	-1.43407
25	0.42739	0.13770	-1.37602	0.40007	-0.04185	-1.44067
26	0.45064	0.13853	-1.37191	0.42620	-0.04205	-1.44679
27	0.47557	0.13898	-1.36446	0.45081	-0.04178	-1.45033
28	0.50093	0.13859	-1.36016	0.47570	-0.04118	-1.45860
29	0.55064	0.13536	-1.34695	0.50049	-0.04005	-1.46611
30	0.60076	0.12882	-1.35673	0.55087	-0.03652	-1.47728
31	0.65107	0.11923	-1.37184	0.60010	-0.03117	-1.46263
32	0.70123	0.10699	-1.38329	0.65030	-0.02427	-1.45066
33	0.75134	0.09263	-1.39177	0.70086	-0.01658	-1.44315
34	0.80102	0.07689	-1.40473	0.74859	-0.00922	-1.43019
35	0.85162	0.05925	-1.41459	0.80061	-0.00188	-1.41649
36	0.90217	0.03997	-1.42814	0.85146	0.00344	-1.40728
37	0.92158	0.03213	-1.43109	0.90126	0.00616	-1.39663
38	0.94162	0.02402	-1.43545	0.92139	0.00635	-1.39153
39	0.96189	0.01586	-1.44189	0.94211	0.00599	-1.38670
40	0.98105	0.00820	-1.44615	0.96156	0.00493	-1.38035
41				0.98145	0.00268	-1.37956

Appendix B. Definition of One-Twelfth Octave Bands

The one-twelfth octave bands were computed as follows.

- Upper band limit in terms of the nth band center frequency

$$f_u^n = 2^{\frac{1}{12}} f_c^n$$

- Lower band limit in terms of the nth band center frequency

$$f_\ell^n = 2^{-\frac{1}{12}} f_c^n$$

- The bands center frequency sequence is then computed as:

$$f_c^n = 2^{\frac{1}{24}} f_c^{n-1}$$

where the "reference" center frequency is 1 Hz (band number 1).

Figure 204 illustrates the one-twelfth octave band boundaries in the 500 Hz to 5,000 Hz frequency range.

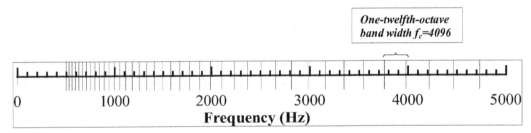

Figure 204. Graphic representation of one-twelfth octave bands

Appendix C. Normalized Noise Spectra

The dependence of the airfoil self-noise with the free-stream velocity is the most critical parameter, therefore the normalized spectra are presented in this appendix. For all cases, the reference free-stream velocity in the normalized plots is 54 m/s. The frequency is scaled using the Strouhal number with the chord as the length scale and the fifth power of the free stream for the amplitude. In these plots the actual free-stream velocity of the data is included in the upper-right corner of the figure.

Prior to normalizing the spectra, the data was corrected for the acoustic losses through the boundary-layer Kevlar cloth, as shown in Figure 11. Note that losses through Kevlar are insignificant at less than 5,000 Hz, for example $\Delta_K \approx 0$ dB. In this figure, the losses due to flow effects, Δ_F, increase with the free-stream velocity; for example, there is a difference of ~ 2 dB in noise levels from 41 m/s (M = 0.12) to 58 m/s (M = 0.17). Thus, the array output levels at greater flow speeds are underestimated. Because the data in Figure 11 below 2,500 Hz are not reliable, an approximate approach was used here to correct the data (*e.g.*, to determine Δ_F in Section 2.2.2). It was assumed that the losses due to flow effects are frequency independent. Assuming an average difference of ~ 2 dB between the 41 m/s and 58 m/s cases in Figure 11(b) (valid for frequencies less than 5,000 Hz), a simple power law in terms of the flow velocity is easily established as $\Delta_F = 2$ dB $= m10 \times Log_{10}(58 / 41) \rightarrow m = 1.3$. Thus, the levels prior to the normalization were adjusted as $SPL_{corrected} = 1.3\ 10 \times Log_{10}(58/41) \rightarrow m = 1.3\ SPL_{True}$(db) $= SPL_{Measured} + 1.3 \times 10 \times Log_{10}(U_\infty/41)$. The acoustic losses through the boundary-layer Kevlar cloth should be measured more accurately, in particular for frequencies that are less than 2,500 Hz.

C.1. Small Chord NACA 0012 Airfoil

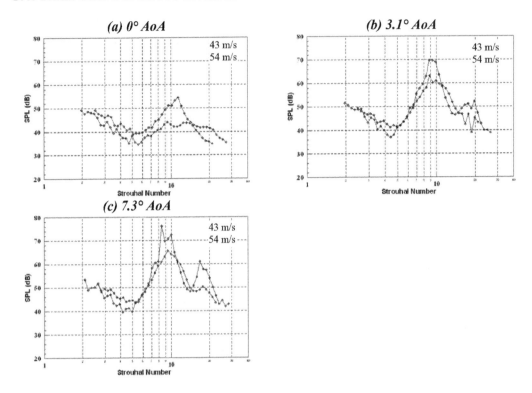

Figure 205. Normalized integrated spectrum for tripped 0.2 chord NACA 0012

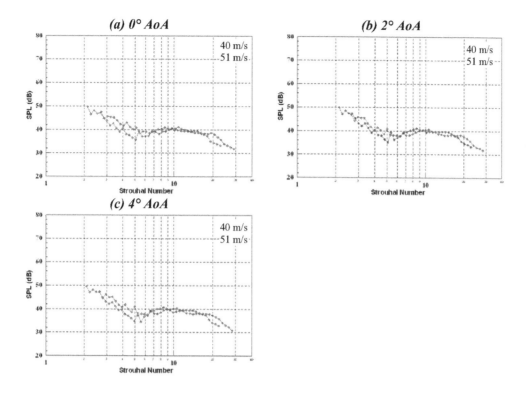

Figure 206. Normalized integrated spectrum for tripped 0.2 chord NACA 0012

C.2. NACA 0012 Airfoil

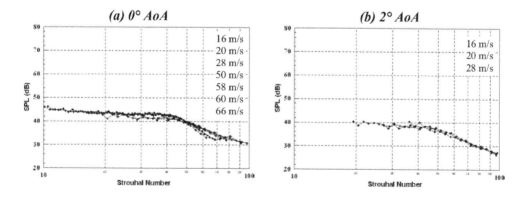

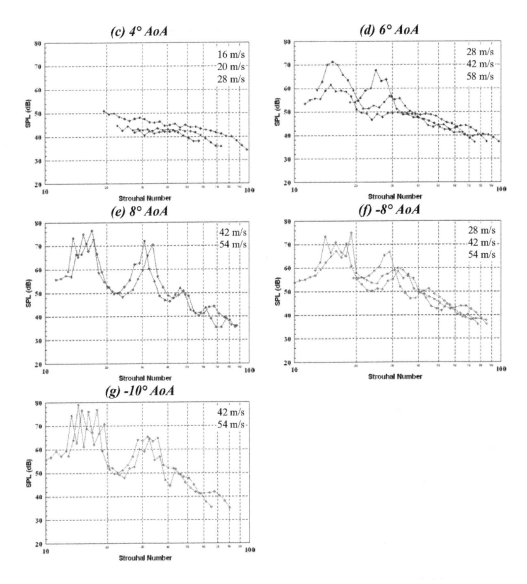

Figure 207. Normalized integrated spectrum for untripped NACA 0012

239

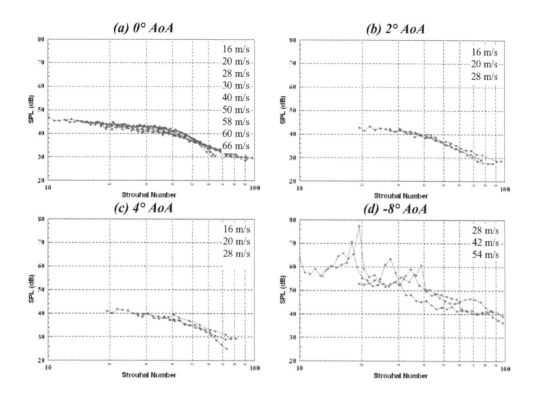

Figure 208. Normalized integrated spectrum for tripped NACA 0012

C.3. Delft DU96 Airfoil

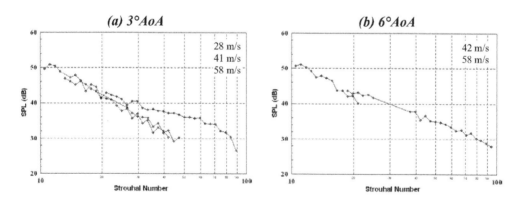

Figure 209. Normalized integrated spectrum for untripped DU96

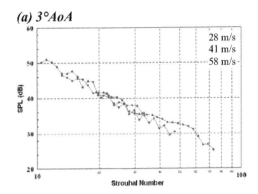

(a) 3°AoA

Figure 210. Normalized integrated spectrum for tripped DU96

C.4. Risø B1-18 Airfoil

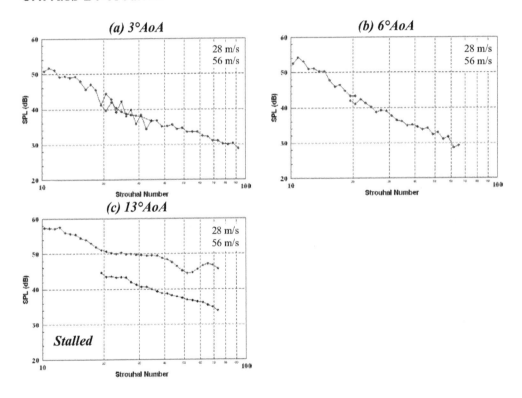

Figure 211. Normalized integrated spectrum for untripped B1-18

241

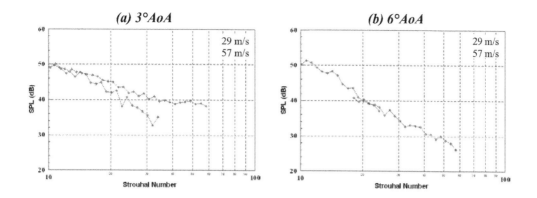

Figure 212. Normalized integrated spectra for tripped B1-18

C.5. S831 Airfoil

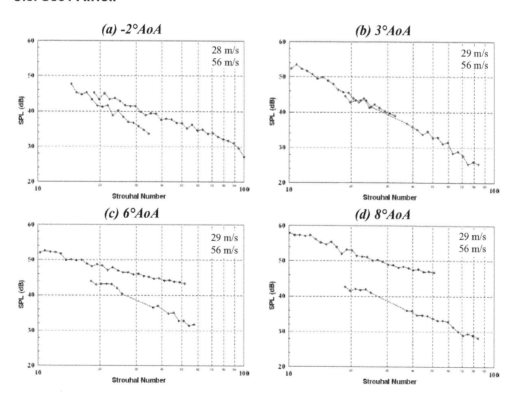

Figure 213. Normalized integrated spectra for untripped S831

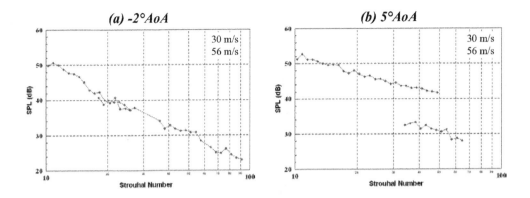

Figure 214. Normalized integrated spectra for tripped S831

REPORT DOCUMENTATION PAGE

Form Approved
OMB No. 0704-0188

1. REPORT DATE (DD-MM-YYYY) May 2010	2. REPORT TYPE Subcontract Report	3. DATES COVERED (From - To) February 20, 2004–February 19, 2008

4. TITLE AND SUBTITLE
Aeroacoustic Testing of Wind Turbine Airfoils:
February 20, 2004 – February 19, 2008

5a. CONTRACT NUMBER
DE-AC36-08-GO28308

5b. GRANT NUMBER

5c. PROGRAM ELEMENT NUMBER

6. AUTHOR(S)
W. Devenport, R.A. Burdisso, H. Camargo, E. Crede, M. Remillieux, M. Rasnick, and P. Van Seeters

5d. PROJECT NUMBER
NREL/SR-500-43471

5e. TASK NUMBER
WE10.3113

5f. WORK UNIT NUMBER

7. PERFORMING ORGANIZATION NAME(S) AND ADDRESS(ES)
Virginia Polytechnic Institute and State University,
Blacksburg, Virginia

8. PERFORMING ORGANIZATION REPORT NUMBER
ZAM-4-33226-01

9. SPONSORING/MONITORING AGENCY NAME(S) AND ADDRESS(ES)
National Renewable Energy Laboratory
1617 Cole Blvd.
Golden, CO 80401-3393

10. SPONSOR/MONITOR'S ACRONYM(S)
NREL

11. SPONSORING/MONITORING AGENCY REPORT NUMBER
NREL/SR-500-43471

12. DISTRIBUTION AVAILABILITY STATEMENT
National Technical Information Service
U.S. Department of Commerce
5285 Port Royal Road
Springfield, VA 22161

13. SUPPLEMENTARY NOTES
NREL Technical Monitor: Pat Moriarty

14. ABSTRACT (Maximum 200 Words)
The U.S. Department of Energy (DOE), working through its National Renewable Energy Laboratory (NREL), is engaged in a comprehensive research effort to improve the understanding of wind turbine aeroacoustics. The motivation for this effort is the desire to exploit the large expanse of low wind speed sites that tend to be close to U.S. load centers. Quiet wind turbines are an inducement to widespread deployment, so the goal of NREL's aeroacoustic research is to develop tools that the U.S. wind industry can use in developing and deploying highly efficient, quiet wind turbines at low wind speed sites. NREL's National Wind Technology Center (NWTC) is implementing a multifaceted approach that includes wind tunnel tests, field tests, and theoretical analyses in direct support of low wind speed turbine development by its industry partners. NWTC researchers are working hand in hand with engineers in industry to ensure that research findings are available to support ongoing design decisions.

15. SUBJECT TERMS
wind turbine; aeroacoustics; airfoils; quiet wind turbines

16. SECURITY CLASSIFICATION OF:			17. LIMITATION OF ABSTRACT	18. NUMBER OF PAGES	19a. NAME OF RESPONSIBLE PERSON
a. REPORT Unclassified	b. ABSTRACT Unclassified	c. THIS PAGE Unclassified	UL		19b. TELEPHONE NUMBER (Include area code)

Standard Form 298 (Rev. 8/98)
Prescribed by ANSI Std. Z39.18

F1146-E(10/2008)

CPSIA information can be obtained at www.ICGtesting.com
Printed in the USA
LVOW03s0104221213

366363LV00007B/441/P